SPECIAL REPORT:

HOW TO MAKE MONEY DURING INFLATION/RECESSION

by the editors of CONSUMER GUIDE®

with

Peter A. Dickinson

HARPER & ROW, PUBLISHERS

NEW YORK

Cambridge London
Hagerstown — Mexico City
Philadelphia — São Paulo
San Francisco — Sydney

1817

Copyright © 1980 by Publications International, Ltd.
All rights reserved
Printed in the United States of America

Published by
Harper & Row, Publishers
10 East 53rd Street
New York, New York 10022

Library of Congress Catalog Card Number: 79–3669
ISBN: 0–06–090782–7
CN: 782

Contributing editor: Peter Dickinson

This book may not be reproduced or quoted in whole or in part by mimeograph or any other printed means or for presentation on radio or television without written permission from:

Louis Weber, President
Publications International, Ltd.
3841 West Oakton Street
Skokie, Illinois 60076

Permission is never granted for commercial purposes

Contents

The home you live in may well represent the best investment you'll ever make. But there are other ways to reap rewards from the real estate market. Here are a few of the best.

Are you single with a taxable income in excess of $16,000? Or, are you married with a joint income greater than $25,000? If you answer "yes" to either question, you should be protecting your money in a tax-sheltered investment.

Paintings, drawings, prints, antiques, Chinese ceramics, rare coins, diamonds, books, letters, autographs, stamps—all can serve as excellent investment vehicles. But you must know what and how to buy. Here are some of the ground rules for success.

Passbook rates have been so dwarfed by inflation that having "money in the bank" is no longer the goal of ambitious people. But you still need savings to cover emergencies. Here's how to maximize the yield you receive on "rainy day" money.

You can exchange your dollars for any of several foreign currencies and/or foreign securities. But you must first understand the potential promises and pitfalls of such investments.

Interest rates, oil prices, presidential elections, labor strikes, upheavals overseas—the investment markets respond to all these happenings. If you know how to anticipate the response, you can make money whether the news is good or bad for the economy.

Here are six model portfolios of $10,000, one each for young singles, young heads of households, developing families, maturing families, retired couples, and widows or widowers. All include something for savings, something for guaranteed income, and something to keep ahead of inflation.

If you follow the suggestions in this book, you should have enough money to pay your bills and stay ahead of inflation.

What An Inflationary Recession Means To You

You're paying more and getting less for your dollar—that's inflation. Unemployment is rising and production is slowing—that's recession. Here's what you can do to make money even when the economy is in a deep freeze.

We're in the worst of times: an inflationary recession. What's that? It's a time when you're paying more for everything and getting less for your dollar. It's a time when you must *save* as well as *make* money just to stay even. And if you want to keep ahead of inflation, you'll really need the information in this book.

How did we get into this mess? It probably started back in 1966, when President Johnson didn't raise taxes to finance both the Vietnam war and his Great Society programs. He did pass a 10% surtax in 1968, but it was too late—increased government spending had started to push up prices about 6% a year.

Money, of course, is politically "sensitive," and in 1972, an election year, the Federal Reserve Board increased the money supply to create a more favorable "pre-election" climate. The result was that more money chased fewer goods and drove prices even higher. Then came the 1973 oil embargo, which raised oil prices in 1974.

While all of this was going on, workers were demanding higher wages to match rising prices. This created the wage-price spiral—one "pushes" and the other "pulls" prices higher.

Throughout this period the government has not helped matters by increasing regulations on everything from safety to the environment. The costs of complying with these regulations makes it more expensive to produce goods, and these costs are passed on to you. Increased costs without increased productivity adds to inflation.

All these factors have boosted prices 6% annually since 1966. And recent events—higher oil prices, rising food costs, increased government spending—have caused inflation to skyrocket to as much as a 13 to 14% annual rate. And while it may recede from these dizzy heights, there is little relief in sight.

What Can You Do About It Now?

What's going to happen? Things will get worse before they get better. Unemployment will rise, production will slow, and prices will keep rising. You and your neighbors may cut back spending, causing business to slump even further. The economy and climate will be in a deep freeze.

What can you do about this now? You can earn 11% or more for only $1,000 invested in savings certificates, U.S. Treasury bills, money-market funds (investment trusts with short-term holdings), and the many other investments detailed in this book. If, for instance, the selling prices of gold and silver increase from $200 to $500 and from $9 to $30 a troy ounce, respectively, you can sell your holdings and make a lot of money. And when inflation and interest rates start falling you can start *buying* stocks and bonds, which should start rising in price. You can even free the inflation value of your house. We'll detail these and other ways to make money later.

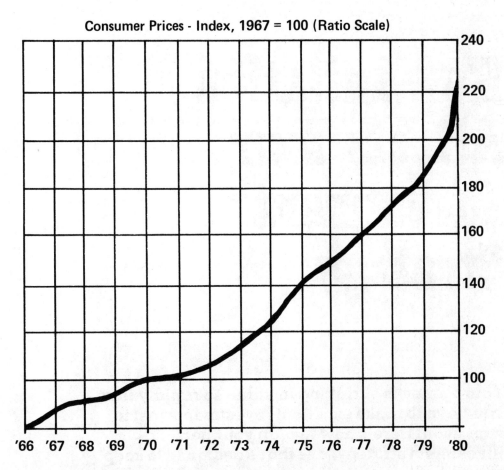

Consumer Prices - Index, 1967 = 100 (Ratio Scale)

Consumer prices have skyrocketed since 1966. With everything costing more, you can't afford to let your investments stagnate.

How Inflation Affects Your Investment Strategy

Your money is shrinking in value so rapidly that you have to make excellent investments just to stay even! Here's how to plan your personal investment strategy, one that's designed to keep you ahead without offering greater risks than you can afford.

Let's look at how inflation cuts into your purchasing power. If you have $1,000 on the first of the year here's how it will shrink at an annual 10% inflation rate.

January 1 of Year	At 10% Yearly Inflation
1980	$1,000
1981	909
1982	826
1983	751
1984	683
1985	621
1986	564
1987	513
1988	467
1989	424
1990	386

As you can see, your $1,000 shrinks to only about one-third its value in 10 years. You must make or save a lot of money just to keep even.

We've already discussed some reasons for this inflation; let's take them one by one to see how they affect your investment strategy.

Interest rates. Your rate of return on most fixed-income investments (including savings accounts, U.S. Treasury bills and notes, bonds, etc.) depends on prevailing interest rates—the rates that lenders charge for money. If individual and corporate loan demand remain high, the Federal Reserve Board (which controls the money supply) tightens the supply and interest rates remain high.

Interest rates affect investments in two ways: (1) how much fixed return you will get; (2) the price that fixed-return investments will bring on the open market. For instance, if you buy a bond with a fixed rate of 8% and interest rates rise to 10%, the price of the bond on the open market sinks to bring its yield in line with the 10% rate.

In an inflationary recession, interest rates usually peak about two months after the recession starts. But when at or near the peak of a recession, there are plenty of pressures, including inflation and loan demand, to keep rates high for many months.

Oil prices. Every 10% increase in oil prices adds about ½% to our inflation rate. Energy prices affect just about every facet of living—transportation, manufacturing, utility costs, housing, etc. In fact, energy price rises of about 60% since the start of 1979 have added about 3% to our overall inflation rate. Rising oil prices (paid in U.S. dollars) also weaken the dollar and strengthen the price of gold (which mirrors the strength of the dollar).

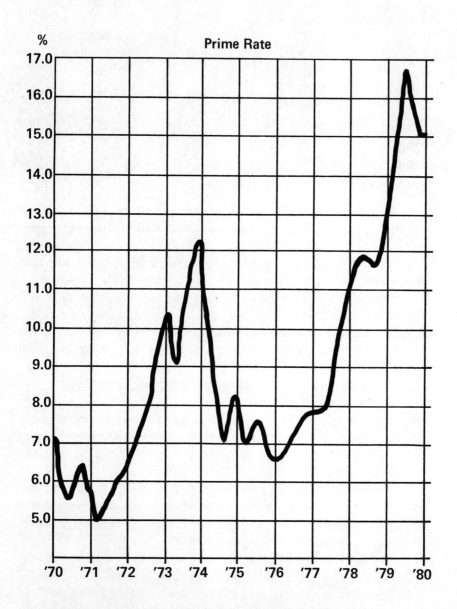

% Prime Rate

The recent rise in the prime lending rate has resulted in record
yields on most fixed-income investments: U.S. Treasury bills
and notes, corporate bonds, etc.

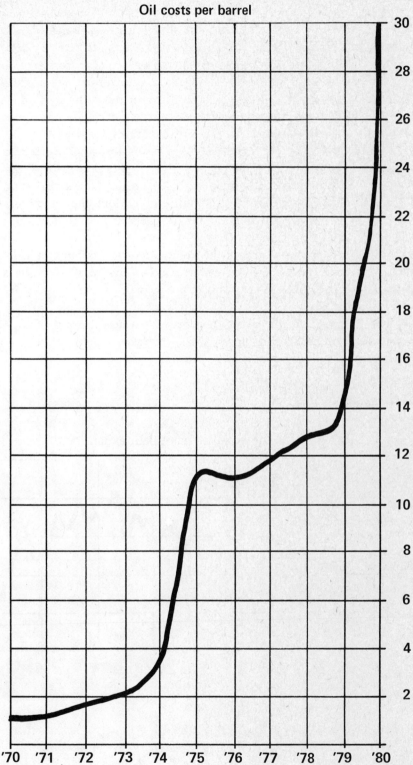

Oil costs per barrel

...e price of a barrel of oil has soared since ...e start of the 70s, contributing greatly to ...r inflation woes, weakening the U.S. dollar, ...d sending the price of gold to record highs.

Strength of the dollar. A weak dollar raises the prices of both foreign and domestic products. Foreign manufacturers (cars, TV sets, wines, etc.) raise their prices to compensate for the decreased value of the dollars that they receive; domestic manufacturers of the same products also raise their prices to match those of their foreign competitors. Each 5% drop in the dollar adds ½ to ¾% to the U.S. Consumer Price Index—and your foreign travel dollar shrinks, too.

Consumer debt. When inflation increases, consumers adopt a "buy now" philosophy in anticipation of even higher prices. If they use credit, they create money that really doesn't exist. All this drives up prices further. As consumers struggle to repay debt, they have less money to spend. Thus, demand for products decreases—and this drives down stock and bond prices.

Weather. Extreme hot or cold weather slows economic production, raises prices and unemployment, and—worst of all—increases all energy costs. Industries that suffer the most are those most dependent upon natural gas and other fuels: chemicals, glass, textiles, retailers, and theaters. Those that might possibly benefit include natural gas companies, propane gas distributors, coal mining companies, oil producers, and nuclear power suppliers.

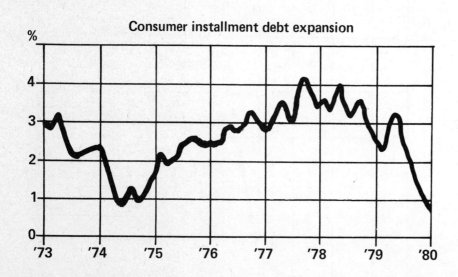

Consumer installment debt expansion

Consumer debt, on the rise since the previous recession, may decline in the near future. If and when it does, the demand for goods will slacken, aggravating the recession (and thereby driving stock and bond prices lower) but perhaps easing the inflation problem.

Political and economic events abroad. American companies and even individuals have a stake in what happens abroad. The Arab oil embargo is just one example; others include revolutions in Iran, Nicaragua, Grenada, and other countries where American firms do business. In many instances, production or business activity halts, and markets dry up. If the new government "nationalizes" an American business, it seldom pays fair market price for the assets of the expropriated company, and the company passes its losses onto the domestic market. A strengthening foreign currency or a weakening dollar makes it more expensive for an American firm to do business, and this also raises prices. And when a country devalues its currency (as Mexico did a few years ago), it causes the value of any local money held by companies or individuals to sink.

How to Shift Your Investment Strategy

Some investment counselors say that when the stock market is rising, invest in stocks and when it is falling, switch to bonds and cash. It's a great theory but tough practice. No one can accurately predict the ebbs and flows of the stock market and interest rates. Therefore, it's best to mix investments, including both "defensive" and "aggressive" types.

Defensive investments are *safe*, earn *income*, and are *liquid* (can be converted to cash fairly quickly if necessary). These low-rise "defensive" investments provide a solid financial foundation that cushions you if your more "aggressive" (riskier) investments crumble.

Defensive investments include:

- Insured savings accounts
- U.S. Treasury issues
- Floating rate notes
- Money-market funds
- Cash value of life insurance
- High-grade bonds
- Preferred stocks
- U.S. savings bonds
- Annuities

"Aggressive" investments, on the other hand, traditionally *keep you ahead of inflation.* These include:

- Common stocks
- Open-end (mutual) funds
- Closed-end funds
- Dual funds
- Real estate (land, etc.)
- Gold and silver
- Collectibles (art, antiques, coins, stamps, rare books, diamonds, autographs, etc.)

These investments are riskier, rising and falling rapidly in price according to present conditions and future prospects. They are more attractive to younger and/or wealthier persons who have more time to recoup possible losses and who have more years to win financial security.

Risk: How Much Is Enough?

Perhaps at this point it's wise to ask yourself, "What financial risk can I take?"

Generally, the younger you are and/or the more money you have, the more risks you can take and the easier you can replace lost money. The older you are and/or the less money you have, the more you should stress *safety* and *income* to meet current needs.

All of us need three kinds of money: *savings* for emergencies, *guaranteed income* to meet expenses, and *investment income* to keep ahead of inflation. Here are how three persons—45, 55, and 65 years old, respectively—might invest $10,000:

TYPES OF INVESTMENTS (in $)

	Age		
	45	55	65
Emergency Money (insured savings)	$ 2,000	$ 2,500	$ 3,000
Guaranteed Money (savings and corporate bonds, preferred stocks, government securities, annuities, etc.)	1,000	2,500	5,000
Investment Money (common stocks, investment trusts, gold-silver, collectibles, real estate, etc.)	7,000	5,000	2,000
	$10,000	$10,000	$10,000

How do various investments to meet these goals compare? The following table gives some general guidelines. The Profile Analysis, which follows the table, is designed to help you determine your financial situation, what risks you can take, and what investments you should be emphasizing now.

HOW VARIOUS DEFENSIVE AND AGGRESSIVE INVESTMENTS COMPARE

Investment	Approximate yield	Safety	Liquidity	Income
Emergency Money				
ommercial banks				
savings accounts	5¼%	A	A	C
time contract	5¾ to 10%	A	C	B−
avings banks and savings and loans	5½%	A	A	C+
time contract	6 to 10¼%	A	C	B
x-month savings certificates	10 to 12%	A	C	A
redit unions	6 to 9%	A to B	A to B	B+
fe insurance				
cash value	1½ to 7%	A to B	A to B	C
oney market funds	10 to 12%	B to C	B	A
Guaranteed Money				
S. Treasury bills, notes, bonds	10 to 12%	A+	A to B	A
igh-grade corporate bonds	9 to 11%	A to B	A to B	A−
unicipal bonds (tax free)	5 to 9%	A to C	A to C	A+[1]
igh-grade preferred stocks	9 to 11%	A to C	A to B	A−
S. savings bonds	6½ to 7%	A+	A to B	C
nnuities	7 to 12%[2]	A to B	C	B to C
Investment Money				
ommon stocks for income	9 to 12%	A to B	A to B	A to B
ommon stocks for growth	1 to 5%	B to C	B to C	B to C
pen-end (mutual) funds	1 to 11%	B to C	B to C	A to C
losed-end funds	2 to 12%	B to C	B to C	A to B
eal estate (REITs, land, buildings, mortgages)	9 to 13%	B to C	C	A to B
nnuities (variable, investment)	5 to 11%	B to C	B to C	B
old bullion	16.3%[3]	A to B	A to B	A+
tamps	15.4%[4]	A to B	A to B	A+
are coins	13.0%[5]	A to C	A to C	A+
rt and antiques	11.6%[6]	A to C	A to C	A

ey: A = Excellent   B = Good   C = Fair

For high bracket taxpayer
Interest and principal
Average annual
Average annual
Average annual
Average annual

PROFILE ANALYSIS: WHAT SHOULD *YOU* INVEST IN *NOW*?

Directions: Circle the answer that most nearly applies to you. Write that number in the space at right. Then add up the numbers and divide by 9 to get a median score.

AGE—My age is closest to:

(9) 30   (7) 40   (5) 50   (3) 60   (1) 70   _____

INCOME—My present income (annual) from all sources is nearest to (in thousands)

(2) 10   (4) 20   (5) 30   (6) 40   (8) 50   _____

ANNUAL EXPENSES—In relation to income, my annual expenses approximate:

(1) 100%   (3) 90%   (5) 80%   (7) 70%   (9) 50%   _____

NUMBER OF DEPENDENTS—I presently have these dependents:

(9) 0   (8) 1   (6) 2–3   (4) 4–5   (1) 6 or more   _____

ESTIMATED VALUE OF ASSETS—My house, insurance, savings, and investments total (in thousands):

(1) 50   (3) 100   (5) 250   (7) 350   (9) 500 or more   _____

LIABILITIES—My bills, mortgages, installment payments, and debts in relation to assets approximate (in thousands):

(9) 30%   (7) 50%   (5) 75%   (3) 90%   (1) 100%   _____

SAVINGS—I have cash on hand in savings or other liquid assets to equal this amount of expenses:

(1) 1 month   (3) 2 months   (5) 3 months   (7) 4 months   (9) 6+ months   _____

LIFE INSURANCE—My life insurance coverage equals (in thousands):

(9) 250   (7) 150   (5) 100   (3) 50   (1) 25 or less   _____

HEALTH INSURANCE—My health insurance coverage includes:

(9) Basic, major medical, catastrophic   (5) Major medical plus basic   (1) Basic   _____

Add up your scores and divide by 9 to get the median. Then consider the questions in the investment strategies that follow.

Investment Strategy Ratings

The investment strategy rating numbers correlate with the *median score* you got from the Profile Analysis. The investment strategy ratings indicate investment categories ranging from (1) ultra conservative to (9) highly speculative. The median score of the Profile Analysis indicates both your present and future financial status and needs. By matching the Profile score (include fraction) with the nearest investment strategy numbers, you know what steps you should take. You shouldn't put *all* your investments in these categories, but these are the ones you should emphasize the most.

1. Insured savings accounts.
2. High-grade government securities.
3. High-quality corporate and municipal bonds, preferred stocks, investment trusts, and annuity income.
4. Lower-rated corporate and municipal bonds, preferred stocks, investment trusts, convertible bonds and preferred stocks, and variable insurance.
5. Higher-rated common stocks and investment trusts, investment annuities.
6. Lower-rated common stocks and investment trusts.
7. Speculative bonds, stocks, and investment trusts.
8. Gold and silver-related investments, foreign investment trusts.
9. Rare and exotic investments: stamps, rare coins, art, antiques, gems and jewelry, rare books, autographs, prints and lithographs.

The above investment strategy ratings indicate *only* the main thrust of your investments. Using that number and the corresponding numbers (if you have a fraction, you'll be between numbers) as a guide where the main emphasis should be, you should then balance investments to assure enough *savings* to meet emergencies, enough *guaranteed money* to meet expenses, and *investment money* to keep ahead of inflation.

Because of rapidly changing interest rates, prices, and stock and bond returns, keep your investment plans *flexible*. Sometimes "dollar averaging" might be the wisest way to invest; other times it might be better to invest a bulk sum and hold it for a long time. Under other conditions, it might be more profitable to invest in fixed income of "defensive" investments like bonds, rather than in growth or "aggressive" investments like stocks.

Investing in Various Investment Climates

You must change to meet changing conditions: interest and inflation rates will change; income and expenses will change. You must be prepared to adjust to the changing winds of different economic climates. The following table describes five climates, one of which will prevail at any given time, along with suggestions for the *growth* as well as *income* investor.

Economic Climate	Growth Strategy	Income Strategy
1. *Calm and steady.* Inflation rate stabilizing at 5%; short-term rates stabilizing at 7% or less, economy rising gradually.	Take more risks in long-term investments. Liquidity can be low.	Invest in quality bonds of 10 years or more maturity.
2. *Cool and clouding.* Inflation is down, short-term rates stabilizing above lows; business recovery gradual but uneven.	Invest in *quality* growth issues that should do well in both up and down markets.	Invest in quality bonds under years maturity. Consider call options.
3. *Barometer falling; cloudy.* Inflation and interest rates up; economic growth rising; environment becoming less stable.	Take profits and upgrade portfolio. Reduce risk exposure. Increase liquidity.	Seek shorter maturities (5 year or less) on bonds; consider call options.
4. *Storm clouds gathering; wind increasing.* Inflation and interest rates rising fast; economic growth accelerating; instability increasing.	Reduce risk exposure; maximize liquidity; shorten maturities; hedge with gold or covered options.	Increase holdings of short-term maturities (under 1 year); roll over if short-term rates remain high.
5. *Stormy and windy with little letup in sight.* Inflation and interest rates at new highs with no relief in sight.	Retain stress on liquidity; buy options in 8 to 12-month range with 10 to 15% of capital; maintain gold hedge.	Move to longer-term maturities at high interest rates; buy call options.

Investing To Beat An Inflationary Recession: Gold And Silver

When the value of paper money plummets, the value of precious metal skyrockets. Here's how to make a profit in the volatile gold and silver markets.

In days of high, even double-digit, inflation, a sinking dollar, and sagging stock and bond markets, gold and silver investments more than preserve your purchasing power. Precious metal prices soar when paper-money values plummet. Everyone should have at least 15 to 25% investments in gold and silver to protect against losses in stocks and bonds and losses in the purchasing power of the dollar.

Gold and silver prices generally rise on "bad news" and drop on "good news." This is particularly true of gold, which is valued as a *monetary metal*, rather than silver, which is viewed as an *industrial metal*. Gold forecasts trends in the money markets. Silver, which usually moves in tandem with gold, has not always paced these moves, but the long-term outlook for silver may be as favorable as gold. Thus, if you invest in both metals for the long term, your patience will be rewarded.

Gold Investments—Why, When, How, Where to Buy

Gold is beautiful, scarce, and imperishable. It is immune to corrosion, rust, and tarnish; it can be shaped without heat and hammered so thin that light passes through it; one ounce can be drawn into a wire 50 miles long.

Any time is a good time to buy if you plan to hold your investment over a period of years, but as the history of gold prices indicates, *short-term* prices are volatile. So, naturally, it is best to buy gold when it's at a low point of a cycle.

Generally, gold prices are *lowest* during *summer months* (when production is greatest, fabricators are closed for vacations, and Islamic religious observances restrict commercial activity); in the *middle of the month* (between gold auctions, which often drive up prices); and on a *Monday* (when short sellers take new positions). Gold prices are *highest* when stock and bond prices are lowest; when the dollar has sunk to new lows; and when oil prices are rising.

Although gold is valued for its monetary worth, it is also influenced by industrial demand, which breaks down (in order of significance) into: (1) jewelry and art; (2) electronics; (3) dentistry; (4) other industrial uses; (5) medals and other decorative uses. Naturally, this industrial demand could be weakest during a recession. In any event, it's best to *buy* on price *dips* and sell on price *rises*.

The price of gold investments is based primarily on the London gold "fix," a twice-daily price quotation. Prices are quoted in troy ounces and U.S. dollars. The London fix (or spot price) is *the* price at which gold is marketed. You can find this price quoted on all-news radio stations and in newspapers such as *The Wall Street Journal*.

Here are major ways you can buy and sell gold.

• *Gold bullion.* Banks, security dealers, commodity exchanges as

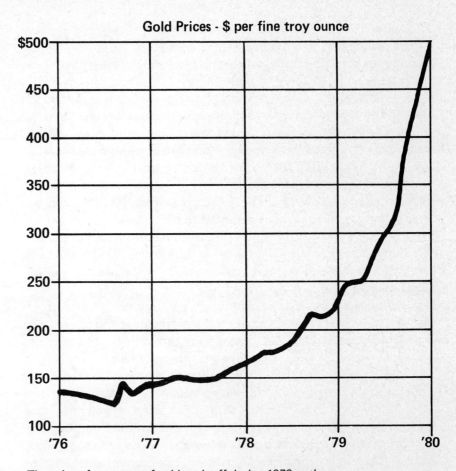

Gold Prices - $ per fine troy ounce

The price of an ounce of gold took off during 1979 as the dollar sunk to new lows and oil prices kept rising. As long as the economic picture looks bleak, gold will remain an attractive investment.

well as department and jewelry stores usually sell some form of gold bullion (wafers, ingots, ornaments) and gold coins. The bullion may cost as much as 8% more than on the London market, and dealers usually charge about 6% on a sale. In addition, banks add storage costs to hold bullion in their vaults, you may want to buy insurance, and you will pay an assay charge when you want to sell. In short, gold bullion would have to appreciate at least 15% a year to make up for all the charges and equal the return you may receive on conventional investments.

    • *Gold bullion coins.* These are easier to buy in small lots and easier to store. You can buy and sell them at certain banks, coin dealers, and some brokerage houses. The most popular are the *bul-*

lion coins, which sell at only a 3 to 10% premium above gold content. Most popular is the *South African Krugerrand* (1 oz., 22-karat gold). In the same class among foreign coins are *Mexican 50-Peso* (1.2 troy oz., 21.6 k) and the *Austrian 100 Korona* (.9802 oz., 21.6 k).

Generally, you would pay about a 6% premium over the London fix to buy these coins and would receive about 2½% less than the London fix to sell them. You can find coin dealers listed in local papers and telephone books, or you can buy through mail-order dealers such as Bramble Coins [1604 Michigan National Tower, Lansing, MI 48933, toll-free (800) 248-5952 or in Michigan (517) 484-3198] and Deak-Perera [offices in major cities, or 630 Fifth Ave., New York, NY 10020, toll-free (800) 223-5510; New York residents call (212) 757-0100].

American bullion coins include the *Engelhard Prospector* (1 oz., 23.9 k), the *Franklin Mint Gold Piece* (¼, ½, 1 oz., 24 k), and in 1980, you will be able to buy a ½ or 1 oz .900 fine gold coin minted by the U.S. Bureau of the Mint.

You usually get a discount if you buy 10 or more coins, and you can avoid sales tax if you buy out of state. Remember, the above coins aren't monetary coins used in everyday transactions, but they are easily recognizable and traded freely on open markets.

• *Rare gold coins.* Coins such as the American $20 gold piece or the British sovereign usually have a premium of 10 to 100% above gold content. Unfortunately, these coins are often faked, so you must have confidence in your dealer. If you buy, deal only through the coin department of a reputable bank or department store or through a coin dealer who is a recognized member of a professional society such as the International Numismatic Society, the American Numismatic Association, or the Professional Numismatics Guild. Most of these organizations offer authentication services, and their members should give you a "dealer's certificate of title, guarantee of genuineness, and registration" or at least a bill of sale stating the coin's genuineness, and a guarantee.

A knowledgeable person to contact would be Walter Perschke, president of Numisco, Inc., 175 W. Jackson Blvd., Suite A-640, Chicago, IL 60604, who manages a rare coin portfolio. You can also consult books such as the *Guidebooks of United States Coins*, commonly known as the "Redbook." It is edited by R. S. Yeoman and published yearly by Western Publishing Co. (cost about $3.95). When buying foreign gold coins, two good books are Robert Friedberg's *Gold Coins of the World*, published by Currency Institute Inc. (cost about $22.50) and Hans Schlumberger's *European Gold Coins Guide Book*, published by Krause Publications (about $25). Books are for sale at most coin shops.

• *Gold futures contracts.* These offer above-average profits, but higher risks. Futures are traded on five different U.S. exchanges and in several foreign exchanges. Contract sizes vary from one-kilo bars (32.151 troy oz.) to 400 troy-oz. bars. You need a minimum deposit of $5,000 to open a commodity account with a broker; once the account is open, the margin on each gold contract is $1,000. For as little as 5% margin you have tremendous buying and selling leverage. For example, if you bought a contract containing 100 oz. (the usual size transacted), for every $1 gold moved up or down, you would make or lose $100. A $10 move would mean a $1,000 profit or loss on a contract. Brokerage commission for this trade is about $50 in and out. You can get further information on gold futures through large brokerage houses and through Commodity Exchange, 4 World Trade Center, New York, NY 10048, or Chicago Mercantile Exchange, 444 West Jackson Blvd., Chicago, IL 60606. If you have any doubts or questions about any transactions, you can call the Commodity Futures Trading Commission by calling (800) 424-9838—in Alaska and Hawaii, (800) 424-9707.

• *Gold depository certificates.* These give you an "undivided but specific" interest in a certain identifiable bar of bullion. Generally, you pay a minimum of $2,500 to get a certificate, but you can make subsequent investments for as little as $100. You pay a 3% commission to buy and a 1 to 3% commission to sell. Assay charge and sales taxes are usually eliminated, although you may have to pay modest insurance and storage fees. And while the commissions and charges work out to about what you'd pay if you bought gold directly on the spot market, the certificates avoid some problems of outright purchase—such as providing for storage and security on your own. For further information, contact leading brokerage houses or Deak-Perera, 1800 K. St., NW, Washington, D.C. 20006, phone (800) 424-1186, or Dreyfus Gold Deposits, 600 Madison Ave., New York, NY, phone (800) 223-5525. For as little as $1,000 and a 3% commission, you can get gold certificates through Citibank, 399 Park Ave., New York, NY 10022.

• *Gold options.* These are offered through certain brokerage houses by the Mocatta Metals Corp. but not sold by Mocatta directly. The gold options operate like stock options, except that the quotes are given by Mocatta, not by options exchanges. Option size is 100 ounces with expirations varying up to 15 months. To open an account you pay the exact amount of the option (e.g., $2,000 or $3,000) instead of the minimum $5,000 required to open a commodities futures account. The commission should be no more than $350, or 15% of the premium. If you wish to sell the option instead of letting it expire, you'd pay a $100 charge.

The difference between gold options and futures is that you are paying from 8 to 15% (premium and commission) instead of about 5% of the value of a futures contract—but you'll never get a margin call. The advantages of options is that you can never lose more than your original purchase price. The drawback is that you pay a premium of about 1% a month, and you stand to lose your entire investment. Mocatta options are the only ones legally allowed to be sold in the U.S. The U.S. government has totally banned all other options because of fraud and misrepresentation. For further information on options, contact leading brokerage houses such as Shearson Hayden Stone or Bache & Co.

• *North American gold mining companies.* These concerns operate in a favorable political environment, and large domestic markets exist for trading shares. However, you have only a handful to choose from, and most produce gold only as a byproduct of other metals such as copper or iron. The leading producers sold on American exchanges are:

- Campbell Red Lake
- Dome Mines

- Giant Yellowknife
- Homestake Mining

And on the Toronto Exchange you could buy shares of:

- Agnico-Eagle
- Camflo

- Campbell Chibougamau
- Sigma

For further information, contact your broker.

• *South African gold mining companies.* These are the most efficient and profitable in the world. An active over-the-counter market exists in the U.S. for the ADRs (American Depository Receipts) representing the shares of the prominent South African companies. These companies pay dividends semiannually—many yield around 10%—mainly because of the unfavorable political and economic climate stemming from South Africa's racial problems. This negative factor may already be discounted in the prices of South African gold shares, but future political developments in South Africa may, at times, exert more influence on stock prices than the underlying price of gold. Here are leading producers:

- Gold Fields of S.A.
- Libanon
- President Brand
- President Steyn

- Vaal Reefs
- West Driefontein
- Western Holdings

Many of these mines offer you a "double-play" in the sense that they also are producers of uranium. For further information see your broker. Also ask about shares of holding companies like ASA Ltd. and Aglo-American, which are traded on major exchanges.

You can also buy portfolios of gold mining stocks (both American and South African) through mutual funds such as International Investors, 122 East 42nd St., New York, NY 10017, and United Services Fund, 110 E. Bryd, Universal City, TX.

• *Gold jewelry.* The largest quantity of gold goes into jewelry. Since pure gold is too soft to be used exclusively in jewelry, it is alloyed with other metals, often silver. Pure gold is 24 karats; 18-karat gold would be 75% pure. Jewelry is usually 10, 14, 18, or 22 karats, but in the U.S. the Federal Trade Commission allows a tolerance of ½ karat and jewelers take full advantage of this allowance. Thus 18 karats is invariably 17½ karats (other countries don't allow this tolerance).

If you want to sell or buy gold jewelry, you must depend upon a reputable dealer—one who has been established a long time. This is especially true if you want to buy for investment or sale. Because dealers charge as much as 300% markup, gold would have to practically *triple* in value for you to break even. And most old-gold dealers will pay only 50 to 60% of market value for gold content. If you sell, be sure the dealer *posts prices* for gold and silver content; this price is usually discounted from the spot price (London fix), so you'll have an idea of how much of a discount you'll get. And since the dealer has to determine the intrinsic value of the gold or silver content, you are entirely at his mercy unless you've had the item assayed or are sure of its true value—which includes knowing both karats and weight. For a brochure showing all different types of gold bar jewelry with a complete price list, write: Deak-Perera, 1800 K St., NW, Washington, D.C. 20006.

Silver—The Long-Term Profit Potential

Historically, the gold-to-silver price ratio is 27 to 1, although year-to-year swings have been wider. This means that when gold was selling for around $300 an ounce, silver should have been selling for around $11 a share, although it did not go that high at that time.

Although there is a steady demand for silver (photography, heirlooms, jewelry, medallions, silverware), the price fluctuates because silver is usually mined as a byproduct of copper, iron, zinc, and other metals and its price depends somewhat on the price of these other metals; because the market is "thin" (small), and any large buying or selling "shocks" the market; and because silver is easily manipulated by governments (including the U.S., which has large holdings, and India, which supplies much of the metal) and even individuals (the Hunt brothers of Texas have been major silver speculators). Still, many investors feel silver is a good inflation hedge, especially considering its

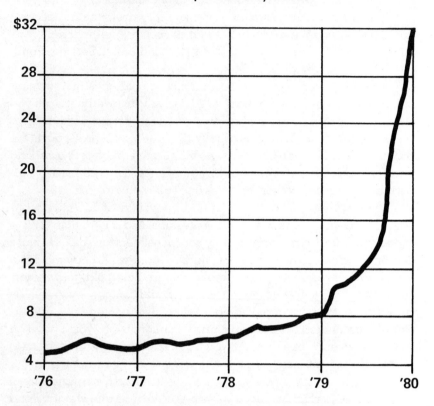

Silver Prices - per fine troy ounce

Silver prices haven't attracted as much media attention as gold prices have, but the rise in price of an ounce of silver has been equally (if not more) dramatic.

appreciation in the last decade. It's available in bullion, coins, futures, silver art as well as silver mining securities.

What's a good *buying* price? It depends on your objective. If you're buying silver as an investment, consider its long-term potential and don't be swayed by violent changes. But also consider that in a recession, the industrial demand will *drop* as will the price.

Here are some of your investment options:

• *Silver bullion.* You can buy 100-oz. bars at a dealer markup of about 50 to 70 cents per ounce, but you'd be better off buying 1,000-oz. bars ($100 to $350 commission). Your bank may lend you up to 70% of the value of the bullion. You can buy this bullion through various channels, including but not limited to the American Board of Trade, 286 Fifth Ave., New York, NY 10001.

• *Silver futures.* You can buy a "futures contract," which states that you will contract to purchase 10,000 ounces (sometimes 5,000 ounces or less) at a specified price. You usually buy the contract at 10 to 25% down and pay no interest. But if the price drops as little as 50 cents an ounce, you could be "called" for the total amount of your contract. On the other hand, if the price of silver rises higher than your contract price, you could sell it for a tidy profit. *Silver futures are risky;* unless you've got money to speculate with, stay away. For further information: Chicago Board of Trade, 141 W. Jackson Blvd., Chicago, IL 60604.

• *Silver coins.* You can buy coins outright on a futures contract. One good point for coins: they can't be worth less than their face value. Dimes, quarters, and half-dollars minted during and prior to 1964 were made of 90% pure silver. Each $1,000 face amount of such coins contains approximately 715 to 725 fine ounces of actual silver content. To figure the premium or discount of these 90% silver coins relative to the silver bullion price, multiply the number of ounces of pure silver contained in a $1,000 face bag—about 720 ounces—times the current silver bullion price, and then compare it to spot quotations for silver bags themselves. The premium usually hovers around 5%.

You can also buy coins in bulk, or "bags," either through coin dealers or investment brokers. Many investors buy on margin, putting down 25% or less and financing the rest at around 10% annual interest. Commissions generally run around 3%, and you may have to pay a "storage" fee for each bag and incidental expenses. Since the average unpaid balance on each bag is usually more than its $1,000 face value, the bags don't fully collateralize many loans, and margin buyers thus face the possibility of being sold out on a price break.

Rare silver coins have tripled in value since the start of 1979 and are expected to hold up better than bullion coins during the recession. For a recent study comparing silver and gold bullion with their numismatic counterparts, send a stamped, self-addressed envelope to Numisco, Inc., 175 W. Jackson Blvd., A-640, Chicago, IL 60604. You can also send for a book, *Modern Silver Coinage*, available for about $10 postpaid from the Silver Institute, 1001 Connecticut Ave., NW, Washington D.C. 20036. And the two long-time "bibles" for collectors of American coins are the *Guidebook of United States Coins* and the *Handbook of United States Coins* by R. S. Yeoman. These should be available at most libraries and coin or department stores.

• *Silver art.* You can purchase bar ingots, medallions, plates, silverware, serving sets, and antiques. Value depends on supply and demand for them as art, as well as for their silver content. Some medallic art is limited—after subscription rolls close, the minting dies are destroyed. *The Franklin Mint* (Franklin Center, PA 19063) specializes in proof-quality sterling commemorative medals, ingots, clocks, and plates. But if you buy, *buy mainly for your own pleasure*, not for profit. A secondary market seldom exists for silver art, and many pieces are selling for less than their bullion content—making one wonder about the artistic as well as investment merits.

· • *Silver-mining shares.* Through your stockbroker you can purchase shares of silver mining companies (sometimes a gold-silver combination) that would share in any rise (or fall) in the price of the metal. Most yield only 1 to 3% and should be purchased mainly for *long-term capital gains.* Among leading issues:

- Callahan Mining
- Hecla Mining
- Rosario Resources
- Sunshine Mining

Like gold, silver is prone to speculative ups and downs. If you buy, buy only through a reputable dealer, buy for esthetic value as well as intrinsic value if buying coins and art, and be prepared to hold your investments through bad as well as good years. As always, buy when the market is down, sell when the market is up. If you buy for the long term and have patience, you'll be amply rewarded.

You may obtain information on buyer-investor experience with specific companies from your local Better Business Bureau or Council of Better Business Bureaus, 1150 17th St., NW, Washington, DC 20036

How To Make Money In Common And Preferred Stocks

Stocks didn't do well during the 1970s, but there are some first-rate bargains in securities that should do well during the decade ahead. Here's a broad selection of growth and recession-resistant stocks as well as advice on how to utilize the expertise of market professionals to your advantage.

How good have common and preferred stocks been as an inflation
hedge during a recession? Before inflation started in 1966, the total
return on stocks had averaged 9% a year for more than 40 years, while
top-quality bonds rarely yielded more than 4%. Now, bonds are yielding 11%, and stocks are averaging a return of less than 3% throughout
the 1970s. And from its high in 1968 to the start of 1979, the Dow-Jones
30-stock index dropped 18.3% and Standard & Poor's 500-stock index
fell 11.3%. Meanwhile, consumer prices rose 90.7%

Inflation and the stock market

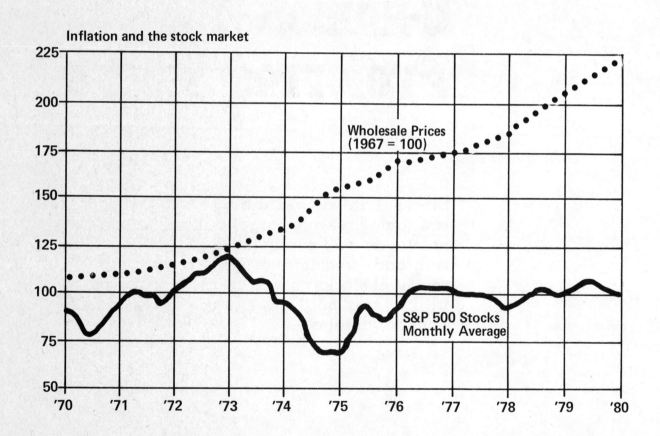

*Stock prices have, on the average, failed to match the rise in consumer prices. For the most part,
therefore, an investment in common stocks has proved to be a relatively poor hedge against
inflation.*

Thus, stocks haven't done too well recently in good as well as bad times. And stock prices could go lower. During the last six recessions, the stock market bottomed out *about 6 months after the start of the recession.*

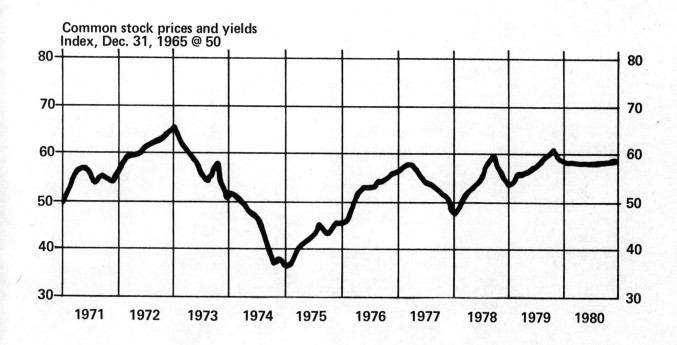

Common stock prices and yields
Index, Dec. 31, 1965 @ 50

e price for a typical share of stock on the New York Stock Exchange declined arply during the previous recession and has not rebounded dramatically since then.

In a recession, the stocks that do best are those of companies that represent the necessities of living — goods and services people need in bad times as well as good, including:

- life and property insurance
- telephone companies
- meat packers
- food chains
- public utilities
- dairy product companies
- distillers
- tobacco companies
- cosmetics
- household supplies

And when the market starts rising companies in the following industries can be expected to lead the way:

- electronics
- aerospace
- machinery
- mining
- manufacturing
- retail trade
- textiles
- crude oil
- chemicals
- paper
- petroleum

Because the recession would place these more cyclical stocks in a good buying range, let's examine some of these growth industries first.

Growth Stocks for the Long Haul

What is a growth company? It's basically a company that is expected to do well over the next several years. It would be a company that

- expands in sales and profits 10% or more a year.
- plows back most of its earnings into research and development.
- has an assured market for its products and a vigorous management.
- has an equity-debt ratio of about 5 to 1 or better.

Here are some established growth stocks that have had 10 straight earnings gains—from 1969 to 1979 (in order of gains):

- Tandy Corp.
- Schlumberger, Ltd.
- Hospital Corp. of America
- Big Three Industries
- Phillip Morris
- BankAmerica
- International Business Machines
- Pepsi Co.
- H. J. Heinz
- Southern National Resources
- Procter & Gamble
- Beatrice Foods
- R. J. Reynolds Industries

What about those companies that might benefit from a synthetic fuels program—developing gas and oil from coal, tar sands, or oil shale? If and when such programs get underway, they should benefit companies that design and build the facilities to produce natural gas or liquid fuel. Among these are:

- American Natural Resources
- Exxon Corp.
- Conoco
- Gulf Oil
- Occidental Petroleum
- Texaco

A company called *Tosco* (The Oil Shale Corp.) also should benefit from any development of oil shale.

What about companies that will benefit from decontrol and higher oil prices? Decontrol of oil prices mainly benefits those companies producing a higher percentage of "old oil." This oil, discovered before 1973, will be converted to "new oil," which will gradually rise to world market prices. Companies that benefit the most include:

- Cities Service
- Getty Oil
- Houston Oil & Minerals
- Louisiana Land
- Marathon Oil
- Mesa Petroleum
- Superior Oil

The search for new energy supplies will aid these drilling and oil service companies:

- Baker International
- Halliburton
- Hughes Tool
- Parker Drilling
- Peabody International
- Petrolane
- Schlumberger

And what about *coal*—our most abundant resource that will play an increasing role in our energy program? The growth of the coal industry will take place mainly in coal used to produce synthetic fuels and in steam coal used mainly in utility plants. Among companies important in this area are:

- Amax
- Burlington Northern
- Conoco
- Diamond Shamrock
- Eastern Gas & Fuel
- Exxon
- Norfolk & Western
- North American Coal
- Williams Cos.

You'll note that many listed are oil companies and *railroads* that not only own large tracts of coal in their land holdings but also are major coal haulers. Other *asset-rich* railroads include:

- Chessie System
- Missouri Pacific
- Santa Fe Industries
- Seaboard Coast Line
- Southern Pacific
- Southern Railway
- Union Pacific

And increased coal production will benefit the following *coal mining machinery makers:*

- Bucyrus-Erie
- Dresser Industries
- Joy Manufacturing
- National Mine Service

Further in the future, *solar energy* will become more vital. Some major companies with stakes in the solar energy field include:

- Exxon
- General Electric
- General Motors
- Honeywell
- 3M Co.
- Robertshaw Controls

What Companies Are the Most Recession-Resistant?

As we noted earlier, the most recession-resistant companies are those that represent necessities of living—goods and services people need in bad times as well as good. Among those are *food companies* such as:

- Borden
- Campbell Soup
- Carnation
- Consolidated Foods
- General Foods
- General Mills
- H. J. Heinz
- Kraft
- Nabisco

And then there are these *food chains:*

- Jewel Companies
- Safeway Stores
- Winn-Dixie

Meat-packing companies such as the following fit in here:

- Esmark
- Kane-Miller

Tobacco companies should also hold up well:

- Phillip Morris
- Reynolds Industries
- Universal Leaf

Cosmetics and *toiletries* will also do well:

- Avon Products
- Chesebrough-Pond's
- Fabergé
- International Flavors & Fragrances
- Noxell
- Revlon

Communications are always used more in a recession. Among leaders are:

- AT&T
- Bell Canada
- Comsat
- Continental Tel.
- General Tel.
- New England Tel.
- Pacific Northwest Tel.
- Pacific Tel. & Tel.
- Rochester Tel.
- Southern New England Tel.
- United Telecomm.
- Western Union

And *public utilities* will always be needed. The following should do well:

- Central & South West
- Commonwealth Edison
- Florida Power & Light
- Houston Industries
- Niagara Mohawk
- Northern Indiana Pub. Ser.
- Pacific Gas & Electric
- Southern California Edison
- Texas Utilities
- Virginia Electric & Power

Selected *insurance companies* should hold up:

- Aetna Life & Casualty
- American General Ins.
- Capital Holding
- Connecticut General
- Jefferson-Pilot
- Travelers Corp.

The *health-care companies* are needed in bad as well as good times. These are good performers:

- Abbot Labs
- American Home Products
- Bristol Myers
- Eli Lilly & Co.
- Merck & Co.
- Pfizer

These other *drug companies* will do well:

- Richardson-Merrell
- A. H. Robins
- Rohrer Group
- Shering-Plough
- Sterling
- Syntex
- Upjohn
- Warner-Lambert

And these companies that are in the *hospitals* and *equipment* fields should do well:

- American Hospital
- Bausch & Lomb
- Baxter Travenol Labs
- Squibb
- Becton Dickinson
- Hospital Corp. of America
- Technicon

During a recession, many railroads, trucking companies, ship owners, office equipment manufacturers, and other companies prefer to *lease* rather than buy equipment. This should help the following companies:

- ACF
- Flexi-Van Corp.
- GATZ
- Gelco
- Interway
- Leaseway Transportation

What If You're Looking Mainly for Income?
If you mainly want *income* with some possibility of capital gain, consider these companies:

- American Brands
- American Can
- AT&T
- Chemical New York
- CIT Financial
- Mobil Corp.
- Southern California Edison
- Sun Co.
- Tampa Electric
- Wisconsin Electric

And if you want both income and capital gains, concentrate on:

- Continental Oil
- Emhart Corp.
- International Harvester
- Pitney Bowes
- RCA Corp.
- Reynolds Industries
- Standard Oil of California
- Tenneco

The following is a selected list of "blue ribbon" companies that have never shown a loss:

- Abbott Laboratories
- Archer-Daniels-Midland
- Beneficial Corp.
- Burroughs Corp.
- Corning Glass Works
- Diamond Shamrock
- Eastman Kodak
- Georgia-Pacific
- Hammermill Paper
- Hercules Inc.
- Household Finance
- IBM
- Koppers Co.
- Eli Lilly & Co.
- Purex Industries
- Standard Brands
- Union Carbine
- Upjohn Co.
- Westvaco Corp.

Let the "Experts" Do the Investing?

If you don't want to buy individual securities, you could buy a portfolio (many securities grouped under one management) through an *investment trust*, either *open-end* (mutual) or *closed-end*.

An *open-end* (mutual) fund is an investment company that issues new shares at any time and redeems shares at any time. The fund is "open" at both ends—buying and selling. You buy from the company or through a broker.

A *closed-end* fund is an investment company that issues only a certain number of shares of its own stocks, sells them, and then uses the money to invest in securities of other companies. You buy or sell shares of a closed-end fund through a broker just as you would buy or sell stocks of other companies. Many closed-end companies sell at discounts, giving you maximum income for a modest investment.

Many funds also offer self-employment retirement plans and automatic withdrawal plans. As a general rule, unless you have ready access to current statistical information and can devote many hours to studying the stock market, you'll get the same—if not better—results from putting your money in an investment trust.

Both open-end and closed-end funds have the following *advantages:*

1. *Management.* You're purchasing management because you feel that experts (who can devote their full time to studying investments and who have research facilities) are better qualified than you to handle investments.

2. *Income.* You get income in the form of dividends or capital gains. You may obtain almost any objective by properly selecting a fund whose investment objectives fulfill your needs. Some funds specialize in income stocks, others in growth stocks, and others in a mixture or balance of the two.

3. *High-grade stocks.* Funds often carry high-grade stocks as a portion or even as all of their portfolios. You couldn't begin to invest in all of them on your own.

4. *Diversification.* Most funds (except those specializing in some industry group) offer diversification that spreads the risk over many industries.

Both open-end and closed-end funds have several *disadvantages:*

1. *Downside risks.* This may vary from one fund to another, depending upon the types of stocks in the portfolio. Also, remember that selling prices depend upon current demand and general business conditions. If you're forced to sell during a business downturn (such as a recession), you suffer a loss.

2. *Administrative expense.* Funds deduct a supervision charge from income before the net income is computed and distributed to stockholders. This fee varies with funds, but in most open-end funds it approximates ½ of 1% of asset value.

Should you buy closed-end or open-end funds? Closed-end funds may have an initial advantage because you pay regular broker's commissions to buy and sell the shares, which may be lower than the "load" charged of some open-end funds (7 to 9% commission, which covers both buying and selling).

However, many open-end funds are "no-load"—they don't have a sales charge—and you can always redeem open-end funds at *current* asset net asset value. Also, if you sell your closed-end fund at a tremendous profit, you will pay your selling commission on a much larger figure than you originally invested. (This is also true for individual stocks.) However, whenever closed-end funds are selling at discounts of more than 10%, they usually are better buys than open-end funds.

It boils down to this: closed-end funds may have certain advantages for short-term holdings; open-end funds may have an advantage for long-term holdings.

Here are some good *closed-end companies* (many selling at discounts) that you can buy through your broker:

- Adams Express
- American General
  Convertible Securities
- John Hancock Income
  Securities

- Madison Fund
- MassMutual Income
- Niagara Shares
- St. Paul Securities

You might also ask your borker about these *open-end funds* that have performed well over the last 5 years:

- V. L. Leverage Growth
- 44 Wall St.
- Sequoia Fund
- Mutual Shares
- Sherman Dean

- 20th Century
- Sigma Venture
- Pennsylvania Mutual
- Templeton Growth
- Lexington Growth

You also can write directly to these *no-load* (no sales charge) *mutual funds* that have done well over the past 10 years:

- American Investors Fund, 88 Field Point Rd., Greenwich, CT 06830
- David Babson Investment Fund, 2440 Pershing Rd., Kansas City, MO 64108
- deVegh Mutual Fund, 14 Wall St., New York, NY 10005
- Financial Industrial Income Fund, 1050 S. Broadway, Denver, CO 80202
- Growth Industry Shares, 135 LaSalle St., Chicago, IL 60603
- Guardian Mutual Fund, 522 Fifth Ave., New York, NY 10036
- Ivy Fund, 28 State St., Boston, MA 02109
- Johnston Mutual Fund, 245 Park Ave., New York, NY 10017
- Northeast Investors Trust, 50 Congress St., Boston MA 02109
- Penn Square Mutual Fund, 451 Penn Sq., Reading, PA 19603
- T. Rowe Price Growth Stock Fund, 100 E. Pratt St., Baltimore, MD 21202
- Scudder Special Fund, 175 Federal St., Boston, MA 02110
- Windsor Fund, P.O. Box 1100, Valley Forge, PA 19482

You can check the performance of mutual funds by getting (from your broker or librarian) the *Forbes* mutual fund ratings published midyear, the July issue of *Fundscope*, reports in *Barron's*, Wiesenberger's *Investment Companies*, and/or *Johnson's Investment Company Charts*. For a free list of member firms, write:

- Investment Company Institute, 1775 K. St., NW, Washington, DC 20006
- No-Load Mutual Fund Association, Valley Forge Colony Bldg., Valley Forge, PA 19481

Another type of fund you might investigate is *dual funds*. Dual funds were established in the 1960s to provide high current income to one class of holder and capital gains potential for more aggressive investors. Since then, the income shares have averaged a yield of 8¼% annually, but the capital shares have fallen with the market and are selling at discounts of 20% and more. Even if the funds stood still between now and maturity (most funds will mature between 1982 and 1985), the shares still stand to regain the discount and more. And should the discounts narrow and/or the market advance, you could gain even more leverage. Some of the leading dual funds are:

- Gemini fund
- Hemisphere Fund
- Income & Capital Shares
- Leverage Fund of Boston
- Putnam Duofund
- Scudder Duo-Vest

For more information on dual funds, see your broker or write to Loring Corporate Services, 74 Trinity Place, New York, NY 10006.

Another possibility is options. Options give you the right to buy (*call*) or sell (*put*) a set number of shares of a specific common stock at a predetermined price for a limited period of time (not more than 9 months on listed options).

How To Make Money Using Options

The price at which you have the option to buy or sell a stock is called the *exercise* or *striking* price; the *premium* is what you pay for the option itself—the right to buy or sell the stock at a fixed price for a set period of time.

Here is how it would save you money in buying (*calling*) a stock. Let's say you think that Stock A will climb from its present price of, say, $50 to $70 in 6 months. If you are right and if you had bought the stock outright, you would have made $2,000 on 100 shares costing $5,000, or a 40% return (before commissions). If you had bought the stock on margin, the return on your $2,500 investment would have been 80% (before commission and interest on the margin loan).

However, if you bought an option call at 7 (entitling you to buy 100 shares prior to the expiration date), you would have had to put up only the $700 premium (plus commission). Had you exercised the call at $70, your gross profit would have been $2,000 less the $700 cost of the option, or $1,300—a 185% return.

And here's how a *put* (sell) can make money. Let's say you feel the same stock is overvalued at $70. You might buy a put option on the stock for, say, $4, which, for $400, gives you the right to sell 100 shares of the stock for $70 regardless of what happens to the market price during the exercise period. If Stock A drops to $64, your option to sell it at $70 becomes more valuable and climbs, say, to $10 or a total of $1,000—or a 150% profit.

Some investors are increasing their portfolio income and hedging against further market declines by writing (selling) options on securities they hold (*covered options*). They average around a 10% premium for giving someone the right to buy the underlying shares for a set price for a set period of time. About the only way they can lose money (on paper) would be if the stock declines by an amount greater than the premium income. However, you can always buy back the option, and your profit or loss would be on the difference in option prices, rather than on the stock being "called" (sold).

Option writing is sophisticated; if you are interested, ask your broker for booklets or write the Chicago Board Options Exchange, 141 W. Jackson Blvd., Chicago, IL 60604 and ask for "Understanding Options" and "Option Writing Strategies" (your broker may also have copies of these booklets).

What About the Specialty Funds?

Some funds specialize in certain industries or areas. Here are the major funds in the following groupings:

Real Estate:
- RET Income Fund, One Winthrop Sq., Boston, MA 02110
- S-G Securities, One Boston Place, Boston, MA 02108

Utilities:
- Drexel Utility Shares, 60 Broad St., New York, NY 10004

Gold:
- ASA Ltd., P.O. Box 1724, F.D.R. Sta., New York, NY 10022
- Golconda Investors, 111 Broadway, New York, NY 10006
- Precious Metals Holdings, 535 Boylston St., Boston, MA 02116
- Research Equity Fund, 155 Bovet Rd., San Mateo, CA 94402
- United Services Fund, P.O. Box 2098, Universal City, TX 78148

U.S. Government Securities:
- American Fund of Government Securities, P.O. Box 9650, San Francisco, CA 94120
- Fund of U.S. Government Securities, 421 Seventh Ave., Pittsburgh, PA 15219
- Luthern Brotherhood U.S. Government Securities, 701 Second Ave. South, Minneapolis, MN 55402
- Mutual of Omaha America Fund, 3102 Farnam St., Omaha, NE 68131

Convertibles:
- American General Convertible Securities, c/o SISCOR, P.O. Box 24226, Los Angeles, CA 90024
- Bancroft Convertible Fund, 660 Madison Ave., New York, NY 10004
- Chase Convertible Fund of Boston, 535 Boylston St., Boston, MA 02116

- Colonial Fund Convertible & Senior Securities, 75 Federal St., Boston, MA 02110
- Harbor Fund, c/o SISCOR, P.O. Box 24226, Los Angeles, CA 90024
- Putnam Convertible Fund, 265 Franklin St., Boston, MA 02110

Foreign:
- Canadian Fund, One Wall St., New York, NY 10005
- The Japan Fund, One Rockefeller Plaza, New York, NY 10020
- Scudder International Fund, 345 Park Ave., New York, NY 10022
- Templeton Growth fund, 41 Beach Dr., St. Petersburg, FL 33701
- Templeton World Fund, 41 Beach Dr., St. Petersburg, FL 33701

Insurance:
- American Insurance & Industrial, 4333 Edgewood Rd., N.E., Cedar Rapids, IA 52406
- Century Shares, 111 Devonshire St., Boston, MA 02109
- Life Insurance Investors, 170 Fourth Ave., N., Nashville, TN 37219

Small Companies:
- Baker, Frentress & Co., 208 LaSalle, Chicago, IL 60604
- Scudder Developement Fund, 345 Park Ave., New York, NY 10022
- Value Line Development Capital Corp., Five E. 44th St., New York, NY 10017

Some Investors Prefer Preferred Stocks

While preferred stocks don't give you the safety of a bond or the growth potential of common stock, some types of preferreds might work to your advantage. For instance, you could buy a *sinking fund preferred* that assures you'll get good dividends, and you could buy *participating* preferreds that allow you to share (usually 50-50) with the common stock any profits above a specified figure. A *convertible preferred* would allow you to convert into common stock (usually a certain number of shares within a given time).

Here are some top-rated preferreds to consider:

- AT&T
- Central Illinois Public Service
- Central Power & Light
- Dallas Power & Light
- General Telephone of Indiana
- Houston Lighting & Power
- Illinois Power
- Louisville Gas & Electric
- NICOR, Inc.
- Northern Indiana Public Service
- Northern States Power
- Public Service of Indiana
- Public Service of Oklahoma

- Rochester Telephone
- Southern California Edison
- Southern Indiana Gas & Electric
- Southern New England Telephone
- Southwestern Electric Power
- Southwestern Public Service
- Tampa Electric
- West Penn Power
- Texas Power & Light
- West Texas Utilities
- Wisconsin Electric Power

Preferred stocks rank just behind bonds as senior obligations of a corporation, and both rank ahead of common stocks. A corporation must pay its bondholders first; preferred stockholders next; then common stockholders. In times like this, it's comforting to have *both* high-quality bonds and preferred stocks in your portfolio.

Where Can You Find Investment Help?

If you find it difficult to find a broker who handles small accounts, you, can write to the Investor Service Bureau, New York Stock Exchange, P.O. Box 252, New York, NY 10005.

Some investment firms will handle accounts as small as $5,000. Their fees generally start at 2% of portfolio value per year, plus brokerage commissions. You can deduct the management fee from your federal tax form if you itemize deductions.

Accounts are either *nondiscretionary* (you approve each transaction) or *discretionary* (you let the investment firm make the decisions). Write to these firms to see what they offer:

- Danforth Associates, 384 Washington, Wellesley Hills, MA 02181
- Spear & Staff, Babson Park, MA 02157
- Bayrock Advisors, Inc., 100 Gold St., New York, NY 10038
- Hornblower Asset Management Corp., 14 Wall St., New York, NY 10005

Some banks offer various investment services, including "personalized portfolio service" (or something similar) in which you can choose from about five investment categories and ride with the bank's decision on larger accounts; *nontrust investment accounts*, in which you invest in the bank's own common trust fund, and "automatic investment service," in which you authorize the bank to deduct a certain amount from your account each month to invest in a portfolio of stocks or in one or two blue-chip companies.

You can also buy stock through *discount brokers* who can save you 10 to 30% of Wall Street commissions, although they seldom offer research services or investment advice. Among leading companies are:

- Baker & Co., Inc., 1801 E. Ninth St., Cleveland, OH 44114
- W. T. Cabe & Co., 1270 Ave. of the Americas, New York, NY 10020
- Dis-Come Securities, 1725 E. Hallandale Beach Blvd., Hallandale, FL 33009
- Letterman Transaction Services, 19742 MacArthur Blvd., Irvine, CA 92715
- Marquette de Bary Co., 30 Broad St., New York, NY 10004
- Odd Lot Securities, Ltd., 60 East 42nd St., Rm. 2227, New York, NY 10017
- Quick & Reilly, 120 Wall St., New York, NY 10005
- Rose & Co., Board of Trade Building, Chicago, IL 60604
- Charles Schwab & Co., 120 Montgomery St., San Francisco, CA 94104
- Source Securities Corp., 70 Pine St., New York, NY 10005
- Springer Investment & Securities Co., 6060 North College, Indianapolis, IN 46220
- Thrift Trading, Inc., 223 Northstar Center, Minneapolis, MN 55402

And more than 500 companies offer *dividend reinvestment plans*. Normally operated by banks, these plans allow stockholders to invest their dividends in additional shares for no or a low service charge. Some companies allow dividend reinvestments at 5% *discount*, and some permit you to invest up to an additional $3,000 per quarter without paying a brokerage fee. The discounts raise the effective yield of these already generous (most yielding 5 to 10%) companies about 0.4%. Among some of the strong 5% discount companies are:

- Allied Chemicals
- AT&T
- Carter Hawley Hale
- Empire District Electric
- International Paper
- Iowa Power & Light
- Kansas-Nebraska Natural Gas
- Pennsylvania Power & Light
- Peoples Gas
- Potamac Electric Power
- Public Service Electric & Gas
- Southern Co.

When would it be a good time to start buying some of the above companies? When the market starts a long-term rise. However, over a 10-year period, the stock market has established these cyclical variations:

1. *The spring rise*, which usually begins early in March and often lasts until mid-May.
2. *The summer rally*, which generally follows price weakness prior to vacation period and often begins during the last week in June and extends through July.
3. *The autumn sell-off*, which begins any time after Labor Day and gains strength in mid-October, particularly in a declining market.
4. *The year-end advance*, which generally begins during the last week in October and is especially strong in a bear market.

In any event, it's always best to *buy* when the market has been in a prolonged selling or down period and to *sell* when there's been a steep and prolonged rise. In a falling market it's best to buy on a Friday afternoon—the market might have reached a low point, with investors unloading in the face of the weekend and more possible adverse news. If a stock or fund is rising and the weekend news has been bullish, then sell on a Monday afternoon with enthusiasm is at a peak.

How To Make Money In Money-Market Funds

The small investor finally has a way to get "big investor" return on capital with a minimum of risk: money-market funds. Here's how to get in on the high yields presently available on short-term deposits.

Money-market (or management) funds invest in short-term (usually under 1-year) securities, including U.S. Treasury bills, bank certificates of deposit, and commercial paper (business and corporate I.O.U.s). These investments are geared to short-term interest rates. If the current rate is 12 to 13%, the net return (after management fee) will be between 10 and 11%. Minimum investment is $1,000.

These funds are best for "parking" money for short periods of time. When interest rates start falling, most investors redeem their money, and management might reach for higher (and riskier) yields. But now they offer one of the best havens for high yields on short-term deposits.

Money Market funds' assets (Billion dollars)

The combined assets of money-market funds have soared during the past two years as investors looked for better yields on short-term deposits than they could get from commercial banks or savings associations.

Most money-market funds offer check-writing privileges ($250 to $500 minimum) and instant mail or telephone redemption.

Among leading funds are:

- Capital Preservation Fund, 459 Hamilton Ave., Palo Alto, CA 94301

- Dreyfus Management, Inc., 767 Fifth Ave., New York, NY 10022
- Federated Money Market Fund, 421 Seventh Ave., Pittsburgh, PA 15219
- Fidelity Daily Income, 82 Devonshire St., Boston, MA 02109
- Intercapital Liquid Assets, One Battery Park, New York, NY 10004
- Kemper Money Market Fund, 120 S. LaSalle St., Chicago, IL 60603
- Merrill Lynch Ready Assets, 165 Broadway, New York, NY 10080
- Oppenheimer Monetary Bridge, One New York Plaza, New York, NY 10004
- Paine Webber Cashfund, 140 Broadway, New York, NY 10005
- Rowe Price Prime Reserve, 100 E. Pratt St., Baltimore, MD 21202
- Scudder Cash Investment Trust, 175 Federal St., Boston, MA 02110

Write for a prospectus.

Stick with these funds as long as they are offering rates that are higher than saving deposits. However, when interest rates begin to fall, then it's time to bail out.

An alternative might be *floating rate notes* issued by many banks and leading manufacturers. Many come in $1,000 denominations, have rates adjusted every 6 months to an average of 1% above Treasury bill rates, have minimum rates or conversion rights, and can often be redeemed at par on adjustment dates. No matter which way interest rates go, you have the downside protection of a short-term investment and the upside potential of a long-term bond.

Here are some floating rate notes issued by leading banks and corporations:

- Chemical New York '04
- Citcorp '89
- Continental Illinois '87
- First International Bankshares '87
- Manufacturers Hanover '09
- Standard Oil of Indiana '89

For short-term profits, you could also buy long-term, high quality bonds at a discount. Many bonds issued by the Bell System and by leading oil and manufacturing companies are yielding close to 10%. When the interest rates decline, *prices will rise* allowing you to take capital gains later. In fact, experts say that—assuming interest rates will have fallen—you can gain 15 to 18% (combined interest and capital gains) by following this strategy.

Here are some long-term bonds to consider for short-term yields:

Issue

AT&T 3-7/8s, July 1990
GMAC 4-7/8s, December 1990
South Central Bell 9-5/8s, March 2019
Standard Oil of Indiana 9.2s, July 2004

For further details, see your broker or leading commercial bank.

How To Make Money In Government Securities

U.S. Treasury issues—bills, notes, and bonds—
are the safest investment issues around. When
interest rates are high, these government
securities are also attractive for their substantial
yields. Here's a rundown on what to buy and how
to buy securities from Uncle Sam.

The government is a massive borrower as well as lender. But as long as Uncle Sam is the only one able to print money, you're assured of getting paid back—though perhaps it will be in cheaper dollars. The government borrows money through several instruments.

Right now, *U.S. Treasury issues*—bills, notes, and bonds—are yielding over 11%. Because they are exempt from state and local taxes, their effective yield is even higher—and they are the safest investments around, backed by the "full faith and credit" of the U.S. government.

U.S.Treasury bills (T-bills) are auctioned each Monday (unless it's a holiday) to mature in 91 or 182 days. One-year (52-week) bills are auctioned every four weeks. They are sold in $10,000 denominations, although you can buy a portfolio of these and other government securities for as little as $1,000 (see below).

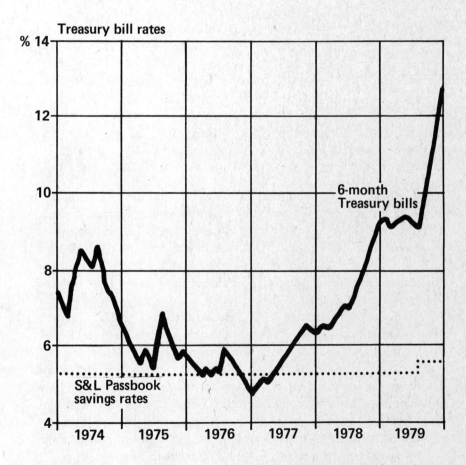

Investing in a Treasury bill offers a far higher yield (with essentially no risk) than putting the same money in a passbook account at a savings and loan association.

U.S. Treasury notes are auctioned each quarter (late in the second month or early in the third month) to mature in 2 to 7 years (generally). You can buy these for as little as $5,000 each.

U.S. Treasury bonds are auctioned in January and July to mature in 7 or more years. You can buy these for as little as $1,000.

If you buy these through a broker or commercial bank, you may pay as much as $35 per transaction. But you can buy *new issues without charge* by submitting "noncompetitive tenders" at your nearest Federal Reserve Bank. The Federal Reserve has branches in many major cities; here are the main branches:

- *Boston*—600 Atlantic Ave., Boston, MA 02106
- *New York*—33 Liberty St., New York, NY 10045
- *Philadelphia*—100 N. 6th, Philadelphia, PA 19101
- *Cleveland*—1455 East Sixth St., Cleveland, OH 44101
- *Richmond*—100 North Ninth St., Richmond, VA 23213
- *Atlanta*—104 Marietta St. N.W., Atlanta, GA 30303
- *Chicago*—230 LaSalle St., Chicago, IL 60690
- *St. Louis*—411 Locust St., P.O. Box 422, St. Louis, MO 63166
- *Minneapolis*—250 Marquette Ave., Minneapolis, MN 55440
- *Kansas City*—925 Grand Ave., Kansas City, MO 64198
- *Dallas*—400 South Akard St., Dallas, TX 75222
- *San Francisco*—400 Sansome St., San Francisco, CA 94120

Write or call for information about submitting bids. You can also write to Bureau of the Public Debt, Securities Transaction Branch, Room 2134, U.S. Treasury Building, Washington, DC 20226 and ask for the booklet, "U.S. Securities Available to Investors" (PD 800-A). Most major brokerage houses also have booklets on buying these securities (although they don't mention you can buy new issues free from the Federal Reserve Bank).

Federal Agency issues—bonds issued by the Federal Land Banks, the Federal Home Banks, the Federal National Mortgage Association, the Federal Intermediate Credit Banks, and the Bank for Cooperatives sell for as little as $1,000 and *yield a bit more* than the Treasury issues because the Federal Agency issues lack the specific backing of the government. However, for all practical purposes they are as safe as their issuing agencies, and no bonds have been defaulted. You buy these issues through commercial banks and brokers who can get them for minimal charge through the American Stock Exchange.

You can also buy for as little as $1,000 shares in mutual funds that have portfolios of U.S. Treasury and Federal Agency issues. Among those (mentioned earlier):

- Capital Preservation Fund, 459 Hamilton Ave., Palo Alto, CA 94301
- American Fund of Government Securities, P.O. Box 9650, San Francisco, CA 94120
- Fund of U.S. Government Securities, 421 Seventh Ave., Pittsburg, PA 15219

Through commercial banks and brokers you can also buy *Flower Bonds*—special U.S. Treasury bonds that can be applied at par against estate tax liabilities even though you buy them at a discount.

However, the supply of these bonds is shrinking because the government has not issued any new ones in a while and because the 1978 Revenue Act has made these bonds more favorable for estate tax purposes.

If you can buy one, seek those bonds with the deepest discounts possible, so you'll realize maximum tax advantages. But since you don't know how long you must hold them, seek high yields as well.

Interest-Rate Futures Markets to Hedge or Speculate

Interest rates will continue rising as long as inflation fears persist. But at some time interest rates will drop. One way to hedge against these rising and falling rates (and falling and rising prices) is to *sell* (or buy) short-term T-bill futures selling at higher (or lower) prices than longer-term T-bill futures. If rates rise (or fall) prices will drop (or rise) and you can buy back (or sell) the contract at a lower price. Your profit is the difference in price between selling and buying.

Because Treasury bills are considered the world's safest investments, you could open a margin account for as little as $5,000 and buy a $1 million contract in T-bill futures for as little as $1,500. But for every 50 basis points ($\frac{1}{2}$ of 1%) that prices went against you, you could be liable for a margin call of $1,250. Thus, you must have some reserve capital to protect yourself against calls, and you should buy or sell futures only with money you can risk.

You can also hedge on interest rates through futures in commercial paper and U.S. Treasury bonds. For further details contact leading brokerage houses or write Public Information & Marketing Dept., Chicago Mercantile Exchange, 444 West Jackson Blvd., Chicago, IL 60606.

A New Look to an Old Security— U.S. Savings Bonds

As of January 2, 1980 the U.S. Treasury began issuing EE and HH Bonds to replace the old "Es" and "Hs." As of that date, the lowest denomination issued will be $50, and the effective yield will be 7% on EE bonds if held to maturity.

The EE bonds will be sold at 50% of face value and will mature in 11 years and nine months. Investors will be able to purchase up to $15,000 in EE bonds each year, but all must be held for at least 6 months.

The HH bonds pay interest semiannually and are sold at par value in $500, $1,000, $5,000, and $10,000 denominations and mature in 10 years. (Their effective yield is 6½% if held to maturity.)

Savings bonds are exempt from state and local income and personal property taxes, but not federal income tax. The interest is taxable at ordinary income levels, not as capital gains. But you can defer taxes on EE bonds by exchanging them (at maturity) for HH bonds. You would then pay tax when the HH bonds matured.

For further information, write U.S. Savings Bond Division, Treasury Dept., Washington, DC 20206.

While U.S. Savings Bonds are best for building nest eggs to finance a college education or retirement, Federal Agency and U.S. Treasury issues offer high current income, safety, and shorter maturities. If you have any doubts as to where to invest any spare cash, you can hardly go wrong with a *13-week Treasury bill*. If interest rates remain high, you can roll over the bill and get the continued high rate. If rates begin to drop, you can cash in your bill and go into higher-yielding longer-term bonds and other fixed income securities detailed in the next chapter.

How To Make Money In Other Fixed-Income Investments

Until recently, bonds were never considered high-yield investments. But that's all changed now. As long as interest rates are high, the yields on bonds will be high too. Here's how to take advantage of the lucrative possibilities in fixed-income investments.

Bonds should form the foundation of your *guaranteed income* program. They can substitute for savings accounts, especially when they are yielding two or three percentage points above savings.

Bonds are senior obligations of a company, issued to raise money for capital expenditures such as buying new equipment, building new facilities, expanding business, or retiring previous bond issues. When you "lend" an issuer your money (usually in $1,000 multiples), you get a fixed rate of return according to prevailing interest rates and projected inflation rates (that's why bonds yield around 11% now when interest rates are high). But if interest rates fall, the price usually rises (and vice versa) to bring the current yield to about the prevailing inflation-interest rate. To figure a bond's current return, divide the dollar amount of interest by the price of the bond. Let's say you buy a

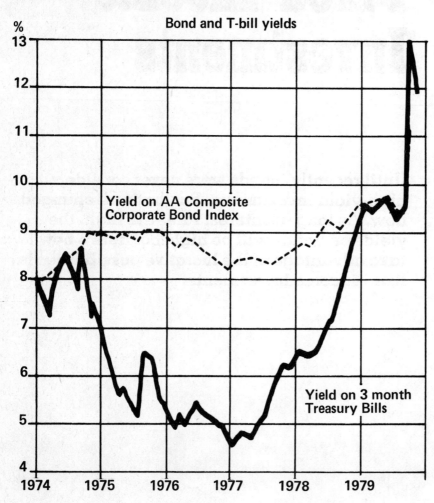

AA-rated corporate bonds are paying record yields, as are three-month Treasury bills.

bond with a coupon rate of 8.5% for $900. You divide the interest ($85) by the price ($900) to arrive at a current yield of 9.44%

You should also consider the *yield to maturity*. This is the total return you'd get if you held the bond to maturity. This takes into account interest paid from purchase to maturity date, as well as any capital gains you might make. For instance, if you pay $900 for a $1,000 bond, you will gain $100 when the bond matures. You then distribute that gain ($100) over the years to maturity (say 10) and you'd have an additional 1.1% yield each year. The $100 gain is a long-term capital gain that is not taxed as earned income.

If you plan to spend the interest from the bond as it's paid, then you'd be more interested in *current yield*. If you plan to reinvest interest, then *yield to maturity* is more significant.

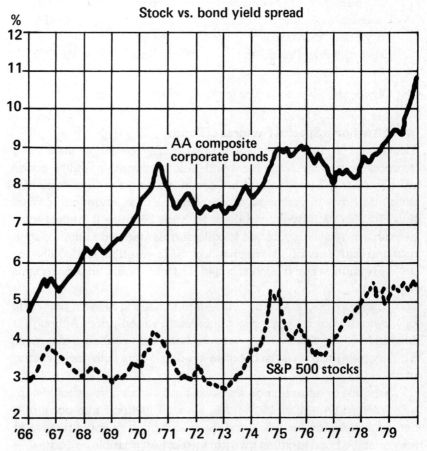

Stock vs. bond yield spread

AA-rated corporate bonds have provided, on the average, a greater yield than typical stocks have returned for well over a decade. Remember, though, that stocks can provide both price appreciation and yield, resulting in a potentially greater total return than the yields on bonds.

Corporations back their bonds in two different ways: (1) *mortgage bonds* that are backed by a lien on property or plant facility or (2) *debentures*, usually backed by a company's total assets, including its ability to make enough to cover interest and principal. The difference isn't as important as the *rating* given the bonds by two independent services, Moody's and Standard & Poor's.

Here are the symbols they use to rate bonds:

Quality of Investment	Moody's	S & P
Prime Investment Grade	Aaa	AAA
High Grade	Aa	AA
Medium Grade	A	A
Minimum Investment Grade	Baa	BBB
Speculative Grade	Ba	BB
Very Speculative Grade	B	B
Extremely Poor Prospects	Caa	CCC

Obviously, it's wise to stick to bonds rated A or better.

What Are Some Special Features of Bonds?

Most bonds have a *call* price or date (at what price or date the issuing company can buy back the bond before maturity). Utility bonds usually offer a 5-year refund protection; industrial and finance corporations have 10 years; government bonds offer longer call protection. You should understand these features because if interest rates decline, an issuer may decide to call bonds issued at a higher coupon rate and issue new bonds which reflect the lowered rates. Usually you get a premium when a bond is called, but you should understand this provision.

Also ask about a *sinking fund*—a fund used to redeem part of all bonds each year by paying bondholders a stated price. Although a sinking fund increases the chances of a bond being called, it also gives a safety margin to an issue because it reduces debt with each passing year.

Because of refunding and sinking-fund clauses, you should consider a third type of yield: *yield to worst*. This takes into account a bond's current market price and the dollar amount you'd receive in interest if the bond is called away at the earliest possible call date.

Buying less that 5 to 10 bonds might cost you a stiff commission rate that cuts into your yields, and you might be better off buying bonds through closed or open-end funds (see below) in which you can buy a portfolio of bonds for as little as $1,000 initial investment.

Good Buys in Closed-End and Open-End Bond Funds
Closed-end bond funds, which are traded on the open market, are currently selling at an average 10% discount from net asset value per share. This gives you more income per dollar invested—in many cases yields approaching 15%. Ask your broker for details on these closed-end bond funds:

- Ft. Dearborn Income
- Intercapital Income
- John Hancock Income
- John Hancock Investors
- Montgomery Street Income
- St. Paul
- State Mutual
- Transamerican Income

You can also get generous yields (often 10% and more) from some of these *no-load* (no sales charge) open-end (mutual) funds. Write for prospectuses from:

- American Investors Income Fund, 88 Field Point Rd., Greenwich, CT 06830
- Dreyfus Special Income Fund, 767 Fifth Ave., New York, NY 10022
- Northeast Investors Trust, 50 Congress St., Boston, MA 02109
- Rowe Price New Income Fund, 100 E. Pratt St., Baltimore, MD 21202

You can also buy *self-liquidating bond funds* (unit trusts) from leading brokerage houses. For a minimum $1,000 investment and a sales charge of 3½ to 4½% you get a portfolio of high-grade bonds that self-liquidate (mature) over a number of years. As the various bonds mature, you get distributions, but as the process of attrition continues, you receive less money.

Don't Overlook Discount Bonds
Discount bonds sell for less than face value for two reasons: (1) they were issued when interest rates were lower, so their price has dropped to bring their current yield into line with prevailing rates (2) the bonds are (or have become) more speculative and their ratings are lower (or has been lowered). These are sometimes called "junk bonds."

However, these bonds can be good buys if they mature in a year when you would have little or no income (such as a retirement year). You'd get full face value when the bonds matured, and you'd pay taxes at favorable capital gains rates. Meanwhile, you could be collecting some high current income.

To spread the risk, you could buy (for as little as $1,000) shares in high yield (and risk) discount bond funds. Write for prospectuses from:

- Federated High Income Securities, 421 Seventh Ave., Pittsburgh, PA 15219
- Fidelity Aggressive Income, 82 Devonshire St., Boston, MA 02109
- High-Yield Securities, 1080 Dresser Tower, Houston, TX 77002
- Kemper High Yield, 120 S. LaSalle St., Chicago, IL 60603
- Keystone B-4, 99 High St., Boston, MA 02110
- Oppenheimer High Yield Fund, One New York Plaza, New York, NY 10004
- Putnam High Yield Trust, 265 Franklin St., Boston, MA 02110

Here are some *high-grade* corporate bonds currently selling at discounts and yielding 10% and more:

- AT&T 3-7/8s, 7/1/90
- GMAC 4-7/8s, 12/1/87
- South Central Bell 9-5/8s, 3/1/19
- Standard Oil of Indiana, 9.2s, 7/14/04
- Dow Chemical 9.8s, 11/1/00
- Tenneco 9-7/8s, 5/1/00

Municipal Bonds for Higher-Bracker Investors

Investors with a joint taxable income of $25,000 or individuals with a taxable income of $16,000 can usually make more money in *municipal bonds* (bonds issued by a state or city). These bonds are exempt from federal taxes and, usually, the state and city of issue. (New York City residents would have a triple exemption.) And *District of Columbia*, *Guam*, *Virgin Island* and *Puerto Rican* bonds are exempt from *all taxes* wherever the holder lives.

In the 32% tax bracket you would have to get a taxable return of almost 9% to represent the tax-free yield of a 6% municipal bond. In higher brackets the advantages of tax-free income is even greater. However, some states like Oklahoma, Kansas, Iowa, Illinois, Wisconsin, and Colorado tax municipal bonds, so check before you invest.

Municipal bonds fall into four categories: (1) general obligation bonds backed by unlimited taxing power; (2) limited-tax bonds backed by part of the overall tax revenue; (3) revenue bonds secured by revenues like toll roads or water departments; (4) housing authority bonds secured by rents and grants from the Public Housing Authority.

Municipal bonds are generally sold in units of 5 ($1,000 per bond). You don't pay a commission, but you pay a markup, which usually averages about ½% on the bond's price.

Some A-rated or better municipal bonds yielding around 6% are:

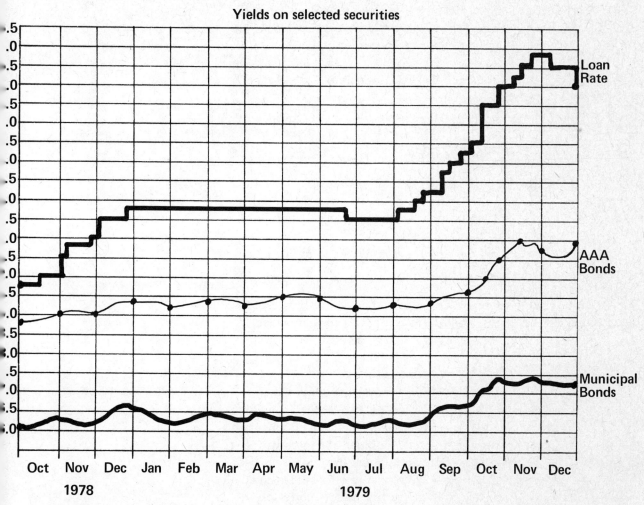

Yields on selected securities

	Oct	Nov	Dec	Jan	Feb	Mar	Apr	May	Jun	Jul	Aug	Sep	Oct	Nov	Dec
	1978										**1979**				

Loan Rate

AAA Bonds

Municipal Bonds

Municipal bonds offer a much lower yield than AAA-rated corporate bonds, but the tax advantages they offer make the effective yield on municipal bonds often higher for individuals with higher-bracket incomes.

- Illinois G.O. 5.75, 3/01/98
- Wisconsin G.O. 5.5, 5/15/99
- Los Angeles Dept. Water 4.2, 10/01/91
- New York State Housing—Mental Hygiene 7.1, 11/01/92

Large brokerage houses like Merrill Lynch, Shearson Hayden Stone, E. F. Hutton, John Nuveen, Paine Webber, etc. usually sponsor *unit trusts* in which you can buy shares for as little as $1,000. These unit trusts are usually self-liquidating and operate like closed-end funds (additional bonds are not added to the portfolio). However, you can buy *municipal bond mutual funds* which offer continuous management of an ever-changing portfolio. Some of the leading funds are:

- Dreyfus Tax Exempt Bond Fund, 767 Fifth Ave., New York, NY 10022
- Federated Tax-Free Income, 421 Seventh Ave., Pittsburgh, PA 15219
- Fidelity Municipal Bond Fund, 82 Devonshire St., Boston, MA 02109
- Kemper Municipal Bond Fund, 120 S. LaSalle St., Chicago, IL 60603
- Nuveen Municipal Bond Fund, 61 Broadway, New York, NY 10006
- Oppenheimer Tax-Free Bond Fund, One New York Plaza, New York, NY 10004
- Rowe Price Tax-Exempt Income, 100 E. Pratt, Baltimore, MD 02109
- Scudder Managed Municipal Bonds, 175 Federal St., Boston, MA 02110

In times of stable interest rates, the *unit trusts* offered by brokerage houses usually offer higher yields. But in rapidly-changing times, the better-managed mutual funds above could be a better bet.

Convertible Bonds to Hedge Your Investments

In uncertain markets, convertible bonds give you the downside protection of a bond with the capital gains potential of a stock. Convertible bonds (and preferred stocks) pay a *fixed income* and can be converted into common stocks — usually a certain number of shares within a given time. The disadvantage of convertibles are that the income isn't as good as the company's "straight" bonds or preferred stocks and the price or capital gains potential isn't as good as the common stock.

But you would have a good buy if the interest rate paid on the convertible is within 1% of the interest paid on the nonconvertible and if the conversion price is within 15% of the current stock price.

In *weak* markets concentrate on convertibles in utilities, food processors, dairy products, and finances. In *strong* markets, concentrate on convertibles in machinery, steel, aerospace, and construction.

Here are some A-rated or better convertibles you could consider:

- American Hospital Supply, 5¾%, 1999
- J. P. Morgan, 4¾%, Nov. 1, 1998
- K Mart, 6%, July 15, 1999
- Georgia Pacific, 5¼%, 1996
- Bristol Myers, $2.00 pfd.
- Consolidated Foods, $4.50 pfd.

You've got to watch convertibles closely. If the stock splits or pays a dividend with additional shares, the shares you convert to should be increased accordingly. If the conversion rate is subject to change or if the issue is callable, you may lose money. To protect yourself you might want to consider *convertible bond funds* like those below, some selling at discounts:

- American General Convertible Securities, c/o SISCOR, P.O. Box 24226, Los Angeles, CA 90024
- Bancroft Convertible Fund, 660 Madison Ave., New York, NY 10021
- Harbor Fund, c/o SISCOR, P.O. Box 24226, Los Angeles, CA 90024
- Putnam Convertible Fund, 265 Franklin St., Boston, MA 02110

Bonds Hinged to Oil, Gold, and Foreign Currencies

If you're worried about tying bond investments to a weakening dollar, you have these alternatives:

- *Mexican Petrobonds*. These bonds yield 10% and more, and their 3-year redemption value rises with any increase in the price of Mexican oil of more than 30% above its level of $13.35 (barrel price when bonds were floated). The bonds are guaranteed by the Mexican government and must be purchased in Mexico in pesos. However, you can arrange to purchase these bonds through most major U.S. brokerage firms. While the peso has remained stable for the last 2 years and could strengthen with higher oil prices, it has had a history of instability. But if the oil price rises 25% over 2 years and the peso remains stable, the 1981 bonds will provide a total return of more than 50%, taking tax benefits into account.
- *French gold bonds*. The French government has issued two bonds (the "Pinay" and the "Giscard") which contain gold payment formulas that relate the interest to the market price of gold. These bonds, which are exempt from French taxes and which are available in units of $1,000 or less, can be bought through most French or European banks. However, as with the bonds above, you can probably arrange to buy them through the foreign bond department of major brokerage houses like Merrill Lynch. Also ask about Eurobonds yielding 10% and more.
- *Foreign bond fund*. Lehman Management Co. (55 Water St., New York, NY 10041) has launched a bond fund that allows you to hedge against international currency changes. Of the total, 75% of assets are in high-grade Eurocurrency debt securities denominated in U.S. and Canadian dollars, Deutschmarks, Swiss francs, Japanese yen, and British sterling. The balance is in other currencies and could

consist of up to 20% in gold bullion. The fund is expected to return about 10% annually; initial minimum investment is $25,000.

As we said at the start of this chapter, bonds should form the foundation for your guaranteed income program. However, because of uncertainties in this period of inflation and recession, *keep your maturities short* and your *quality high*. If and when interest rates start to fall, you can then shift into higher-yielding, longer-term quality bonds.

How To Make Money In Real Estate

The home you live in may well represent the best investment you'll ever make. But there are many other ways to reap substantial rewards from the real estate market. Here are a few of the best.

Good real estate has been appreciating 10% or more a year and is one of the best inflation hedges. You can make money in real estate in several ways: (1) buying *improved property* (land with buildings) that produces income or grows in value; (2) buying *unimproved land* that will increase in value; and (3) investing in mortgages. You have several choices in each category.

What $1 invested in 1946 would be worth at year end; ratio scale

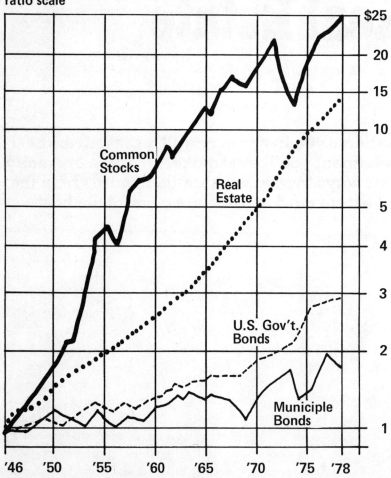

Real estate has proved an excellent investment over the past three decades, climbing steadily upward and not experiencing the recession-induced setbacks that have made stocks so risky.

The Profits in Improved Property

Good improved property has been appreciating from 10 to 40% a year; and it should offer good inflation protection for many years to come. With increasing possibilities and varieties of mortgages (see below) you can more easily acquire some of these properties. Experts say some good income real estate (houses, apartments, land) can be found in these 8 markets:

- Tucson, Ariz.
- Albuquerque, N.M.
- St. Louis, Mo.
- Boise, Id.

- San Antonio/Austin, Tex.
- Columbia, S.C.
- Kansas City, Mo.
- Beaumont, Tex.

Other possibilities include northern New York state, New Hampshire, Vermont, and northeastern Pennsylvania.

Some people are investing in historic properties in Providence, R.I.; Vernon, Conn.; Oakland, Cal.; Boston, Mass.; Savannah, Ga.; and Charleston, S.C. Thanks to the Tax Reform Act of 1979, these investors can deduct their rehabilitation costs over a quick five-year period.

It's also easier to get mortgages to buy *residences*. A well-located single-family home not only becomes your castle, but a fortress against inflationary-recession. Here are some of the new mortgages available:

- *Variable rate mortgages*. These are tied to an approved index, which means future monthly payments may vary and are not known at the time the loan originates. However, the existing mortgage rate may not be raised more than 0.25% at a time.

- *Graduated payment mortgages*. This type of mortgage has scheduled monthly payments that start out at a lower level than the standard type mortgage. These payments then increase over the life of the loan at predetermined intervals to some predetermined limit. For example, a 30-year $35,000 loan at 8.5% could require payments of $269 under a standard fixed-payment mortgage. Under one graduated payment mortgage, payments would be $238 the first year, rising to $290 over the first 10 years, and remaining at $290 for the additional 20 years of the loan. The regulations also set a maximum of 7.5% annual rate of increase for monthly payments. Over the long run, however, graduated payment mortgages will cost more than a standard mortgage. If you want to find out about any of the above mortgages, contact savings and loan associations in your area or in the area you plan to buy property. Not all lenders offer these mortgages; you may have to shop around until you find one that does.

If you're *buying* a home, it might pay you to hire a professional

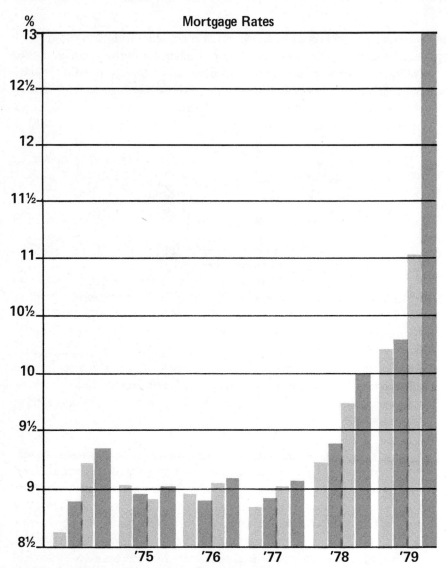

Mortgage Rates

%
13
12½
12
11½
11
10½
10
9½
9
8½

'75   '76   '77   '78   '79

Mortgage rates on new homes, reflecting interest rates in general, soared upward during 1978 and 1979. Nevertheless, purchase of a well-located single-family home remains an excellent hedge against inflation.

home inspector (look in yellow pages of telephone directory) who might charge from $100 to $200 for a basement-to-attic inspection. If you do your own inspection, you'd be wise to send $1 to the National Association of Home Builders, Fifteenth and M St., NW, Washington, DC 20005 and ask for either its "Home Buyers Guide" or "Condominium Buyers Guide" and use their checklist.

Try to get an *insured warranty* on your house, or participate in the Home Owners Warranty (HOW) program. Under HOW the builder guarantees the workmanship, materials, and structure of the house according to specified standards for a year after it's sold. During the second year he continues to stand behind the wiring, piping, and ductwork as well as the structural parts. Beginning with the third year the insurance takes over entirely, covering major structural flaws through the tenth year. The cost—$2 per $1,000 of the selling price—is paid by the builder, who usually adds it onto the price.

If you settle in an area subject to hurricanes or flooding, you should check your eligibility for National Flood Insurance. You can get information by calling (800) 638–6620. Or you can send for the booklet, "Questions and Answers—National Flood Insurance Program," Federal Insurance Administration, HUD, Washington, DC 20410.

Period	Average conventional mortgage rate	Median home price	Regular (20% D.P.) payment
1970	8.40	$23,258	$141.75
1971	7.71	$24,998	$142.72
1972	7.56	$27,110	$152.54
1973	7.98	$30,823	$180.59
1974	8.97	$34,055	$218.62
1975	9.11	$37,237	$242.06
1976	9.05	$41,179	$266.25
1977	9.02	$45,867	$295.77
1978	9.56	$52,242	$353.25
1979	13.00	$75,000	$666.00

Source: FHLBB, NAR, Moody, Jim Kaden—Economist U.S. League of Savings Associations.

mortgage rates went up and the ~rchase price of a home escalated ~ough the 70s, it became increasingly ~ficult for first-time buyers to enter ~ housing market. Homeowners, ~wever, saw their property more ~n triple in value within a decade.

If you're *selling* a home, you can sell it through a real estate broker who will charge you 6 to 7% of the sales price, or you can sell it yourself with the help of a *cut-rate broker* who may charge 1 to 5% for providing advice, handling advertising, and lining up prospects, or a *real estate lawyer* who may charge $200 to $300 for doing the basic paperwork.

If you or one of the owners is age 55 and older and have lived in the house at least 3 of the last 5 years, you may deduct up to $100,000 of the capital gains of the sale (and other accumulated sales). This is a once-in-a-lifetime exclusion, and you shouldn't take it unless you don't think you'll move again or will be hurt by the capital gains tax. You can defer tax on gains if you buy another house from 18 months before the sale to 18 months after. If you build a new house, the period runs from 18 months before the sale to 24 months after. This works only on a house that costs more than what you made on the old one. For further information get the free IRS booklet "Tax Information on Selling or Purchasing Your Home," available at local IRS offices.

You can also invest in property through *Real Estate Investment Trusts* (REITs), which are mutual funds of property investments (real estate or mortgages). As closed-end companies, REITs issue a limited number of shares, which are bought and sold through stock brokers. There are drawbacks to REITs. For instance, during the housing slump of 1974, many buyers refused to pay high mortgage and interest payments leaving many REITs holding empty mortgages or buildings. However, you would have built-in protection if you bought REITs that have mainly properties (such as shopping centers) in their portfolios that are increasing in value. Some REITs are also selling *below book value*, which means they're selling at discounts to asset value. Here is a list of some of the more sound REITs:

- BankAmerica Realty
- Connecticut General Mtg. & Realty
- Continental Illinois Property
- PNB Mortgage Investors
- Wells Fargo & Equity Trust

More speculative might be these REITs:

- First Union REIT
- Federal Realty
- Investors Realty Trust
- Hubbard REIT
- New Plan Realty
- Pennsylvania REIT
- REIT of America
- San Francisco Realty Trust
- Pacific Realty Trust
- Washington REIT

Even more speculative might be a *real estate syndicate* in which several investors pool their capital in buildings or land either as joint ventures or limited partnerships. Participants in joint ventures take the greater risk because they may lose their investments if, for instance, the price of raw land falls. Real estate partnerships have been formed to invest in apartment houses, office buildings, hotels, and citrus groves. Some hunt capital gains or tax advantages, but some sponsors form syndications primarily to earn brokerage fees from the purchase and sale of property. Be wary in choosing a sponsor.

How to Free the Inflation-Value of Your House

Good houses have been appreciating about 10 percent a year, so if you've lived in your house 10 or more years, it's probably *doubled in* price. Fine, but how can you get your hands on some of this inflated value? Simple. *Refinance the mortgage*—a first, second, or "reverse annuity" mortgage.

Let's say you bought a home in 1962 for $25,000 with $5,000 down and a $20,000 mortgage at 6 percent for 30 years. Now the place is worth about $65,000. You replace the old mortgage with a new $30,000 loan, again for 30 years but this time at 9 percent interest (although existing mortgages are higher, lenders will lower the rate a percent or more just to get the lower rate off their books). After paying off the old loan, you have $19,240 in cash. The monthly payments might go from

$120 to $242, but part of the increase will be absorbed by a bigger tax deduction.

If you don't want to surrender your low-interest first mortgage, you could consider taking a *second mortgage*. The rates for this might run from 12 to 19%, plus costs for title examination, insurance, loan fees, etc. The National Consumer Finance Association compares refinancing and second-mortgage costs: A typical borrower owes $31,436 on a 6¾% first mortgage due to mature in 17 years. He wants $8,500. To raise that by refinancing, he would need a new mortgage for $39,935. If that amount were repaid over 17 years at 9¼%, his monthly payments would jump from $259 to $389. In all he would repay $79,368 including $39,433 interest.

By contrast, a second-mortgage loan providing $8,500 in cash for 59 months at 16½% would call for monthly payments of $211. That plus the first-mortgage payment of $259 would mean a monthly outlay of $470 for 59 months, after which only the first-mortgage payment would remain. Over the 17 years the total payback would be $79,368 with refinancing, $65,392 with a second mortgage.

Of course, you could reduce the interest cost of refinancing by borrowing for a shorter term, or you could lower the monthly payment by taking a longer mortgage. And perhaps the cheapest way to tap your equity would be to have the amount borrowed added to the outstanding balance on the first mortgage. This would be possible under an "open-mortgage" clause.

You could also consider a "wraparound" mortgage, in which the first mortgage is paid off on a monthly schedule by a lender who, in return for the low interest rate, gives you a break on a larger loan. Here's how it works: You need $10,000 but don't want to forfeit a 6½% mortgage. You find an individual or mortgage company willing to take over and pay off the loan and advance you an additional $10,000. Although the going rate for a loan might be 10%, he can afford to give it to you at 9% or less because he'll make the difference between 6½% and his rate when he lends you the money.

You could also consider a *reverse annuity mortgage*. This type of mortgage appeals mainly to older homeowners who want to get a return on their major investment—their homes. The mortgage involves annuity payments based on a loan against the accumulated equity in your home. In one kind of reverse annuity mortgage you would sell your home to a lender who would lease it back to you for the rest of your life. Out of the proceeds of the sale, you would buy an annuity from the lender, providing enough to pay rent, sustenance, and household expenses. Other reverse annuity mortgages provide you with a loan based on the equity you have in the home and are to be repaid only at the end of a period based on life expectancy. These plans include guaranteed refinancing at the end of any fixed term, and prepayment without penalty at any time during the loan term. S&Ls are also required to provide a 7-day "cooling off" period after loan commitment. Reverse annuity mortgages are approved by the Federal Home Loan Bank on a case-by-case basis.

If you're thinking of refinancing or getting a first or second mortgage, consider going first to a *commercial bank*, especially if you need $10,000 or less. Your next best bet would be *credit unions* which often offer lower interest rates. *Savings and loans* and *savings banks* do the most mortgage lending, and *mortgage companies* handle most of the FHA-insured and VA-guaranteed loans that carry low interest rates. You could also look in the real estate section of your local newspaper. Many individuals want to make mortgage loans, especially in California, where second mortgages are a big business.

Remember, mortgage lenders usually won't lend you more than *one-fifth* of your monthly income for a monthly mortgage payment. In other words, if your family income is $2,000 a month, the lender will be willing to lend you $400 (total mortgage payments). The lender might raise this to $500 if you have a good repayment record.

Land—The Trickiest Investment of All

Land sells for under $600 an acre in New Mexico to over $2,000 in New Jersey. But the problem with most raw land for sale is that it's available mainly in remote areas of New Mexico, Arizona, California, and Florida. Most people buy for speculation, not building, and the chances of reselling might be nil.

The Federal Office of Interstate Land Sales Registration says it gets some 5,000 complaints a year from people being "swindled" on land deals. Most of this land is sold by developers who advertise in Eastern papers and who sponsor "free" banquets to snare buyers. To avoid getting bitten by a land shark:

• *Don't take "promised developments" for granted.* The promoter may promise shopping centers, recreation areas, golf courses, etc., but he's under no obligation to provide these unless he says so in writing. Also, find out about the costs of any recreational facilities the developer provides. A favorite stunt is to "subsidize" these facilities for a certain length of time, and then lease them back to the owners for an inflated fee. Watch out for "escalator" clauses for maintenance, service, etc. If services are already built, realize that there might be a mountain of debt against the land that you will have to pay off. If services aren't in, realize that you will be assessed for your share: over $10,000 a mile to string power and telephone lines; $6,000 for a well.

• *Find out any restrictions on building, construction, and landscaping.* In many instances, you'll find that any design, construction, and landscaping plans must be approved by the developer. These restrictions may be such that they can be met only by an architect, builder, or landscape designer who must be approved by the developer (who may get a piece of the action). Land use—and the usability of land—also trap the unwary. People buy land only to find that they need more to provide for septic tank drainage or that the land has been restricted for development because the county has put a moratorium on building or has curbed expansion of sewers.

• *Never buy land site unseen.* With a low downpayment and low monthly payments, it doesn't seem worth it to inspect your land. But there's no substitute for a sober appraisal at the land site. Even if you think you might possibly visit the land during a seemingly safe "money-back guarantee" period, how do you know you'll be able to make the trip and meet all the specifications for getting back your money?

• *Try to find out the real value of the land.* It's not uncommon for a developer to resell land for *100 times* what was originally paid for it. The county assessor probably knows the true value. Also, try to find what land is selling for around or near your development. You might find you'd be paying a grossly inflated price for the land.

• *Consider all aspects of buying on time.* The company often retains ownership until you complete all payments. Default on one payment and the company may be able to cancel the contract and keep all your money. You should also compare the developer's finance costs with those of other lenders to see if they're competitive. Make sure you know all about the restrictions, hidden debt, etc., that may encumber a free and clear title to the land.

Before buying, make sure you get a copy of the "property report" the U.S. Department of Housing and Urban Development (HUD) requires developers to furnish to prospective buyers. This report answers *some*, though not all, pertinent questions about the land to help you, but it can't judge or evaluate it for you. If you can prove that you didn't get a copy of the property report at least 48 hours before signing, you may simply revoke the contract within three business days. Should you want out of the contract, put your notice to cancel in writing to the developer.

If you feel you are being cheated, contact the Federal Office of Interstate Land Sales Registration, 451 Seventh St., SW, Washington, DC 20411. This office has obtained refunds in several instances.

The High Returns from Mortgages With mortgages yielding over 10% and housing seen as a prime inflation hedge, shares of private and public mortgage companies are rising in yields and capital gains.

Banks and savings and loan associations—including Bank of

America, Imperial Savings & Loan, Home Savings & Loan—have issued mortgage-backed securities that you can buy through brokers. Leading brokerage houses such as Merrill Lynch, Thomson McKinnon, Bache, and Dean Witter also sell *unit trusts* (shares in a portfolio of mortgages) for as little as $1,000. And you could also invest in private mortgage insurers listed on major exchanges like AMIC Corporation, MGIC Investment, and United Guaranty.

Perhaps the safest way to invest in mortgages is by investing in government agencies like the Federal National Mortgage Association ("Fannie Mae") or the Government National Mortgage Association ("Ginnie Mae"). These agencies insure home mortgages for Uncle Sam, including mortgages insured by the Federal Housing Administration and Veterans Administration. These packages are put together by mortgage bankers who keep ½ of 1% for their efforts.

Among the most popular of investments are the "Ginnie Mae Passthroughs." They are called "passthroughs" because the monthly payments of principal and interest made by the homeowner are passed through directly to the investor. The government guarantee protects you from any interruption in payments.

While the original life of these mortgages is usually 25 to 30 years, their average effective life is only 12 years—mainly because of pre-payment.

You get *monthly payments*. About 92% of your monthly dividend is interest income with the remaining 8% being a return (amortization) of your capital. Minimum investment is $25,000, but you can buy a portfolio of such mortgages through the unit trusts sold by major brokers or through a no-load mutual fund such as:

- Holdings of U.S. Government Securities (HUSGSI), 3200 Ponce de Leon Blvd., Coral Gables, FL 33134.

A major problem with most real estate investments is liquidity. If you need to sell in a hurry, you may have to sell at a loss or wait several years. You should look upon any real estate investment as a *long-term holding*, and you shouldn't invest unless you know the people and the property involved.

And remember this dictum about real estate: the three most important considerations are: location
location
location.

How To Make Money In Tax Shelters

Are you single and have a taxable income in excess of $16,000? Or, are you married and have a joint income greater than $25,000? If you answer "yes" to either question, then you should be protecting your money in a tax-sheltered investment.

Any single person with a taxable income of $16,000 and any couple with a joint taxable income of $25,000 should investigate ways to exempt, defer, or shelter some of their money from the tax collector. (As noted earlier, *municipal bonds* are exempt from federal taxes and usually the state and city which issues the bond. District of Columbia, Virgin Island, Guam, and Puerto Rican Bonds are exempt from all taxes anywhere.)

U.S. Treasury issues, many federal agency issues, and U.S. Savings Bonds are exempt from state and local taxes. And many utilities and other companies offer wholly or partially tax-exempt dividends. Here are some companies that have offered them in the past (there's no assurance the tax-exempt status will continue):

- American Electric Power
- American Family Corp.
- American Heritage Life
- Burns (R.L.)
- Central Securities
- Cleveland Electric Ill.
- Continental Illinois Properties
- Dayton Power & Light
- Denver Real Estate Investment
- Forest Oil
- General Growth Properties
- General Host
- Koger Properties
- Long Island Lighting
- Mesa Petroleum·
- National Life of Florida
- Niagara Mohawk Power
- Ohio Edison
- Pennsylvania Power & Light
- Prudent Real Estate
- Public Service Electric & Gas
- Rouse Co.
- Toledo Edison
- Western Union

You can also shelter money from taxes through *IRA* (Individual Retirement Accounts) and *Keogh* plans. Here is how they work:

- *IRA plans.* Under a regular plan you can tax shelter (if your company doesn't have a retirement plan) 15% of earned income up to $1,500 a year ($1,750 for a working and nonworking spouse). However, a new ruling allows companies to contribute up to $7,500 a year (or 15% of employee's earned income, if that amounts to a lesser figure) in an IRA. If the company's contribution is less than the normal IRA maximum payment, the individual can put in an additional amount of his own to bring it up to the regular maximum. If you leave the company, you can "roll-over" part of your lump-sum pension or profit-sharing payout into an IRA plan and shelter it from current taxes. And you can keep whatever portion of such a lump-sum payment you need for living or other expenses and shelter the part you don't need from taxes.

After	With a tax-sheltered plan	Without a tax-sheltered plan	"Extra" money for retirement
5 years	$ 9,628	$ 6,789	$ 2,839
10 years	24,073	16,020	8,053
15 years	45,740	28,571	17,169
20 years	78,242	45,637	32,605
25 years	126,998	68,840	58,158
30 years	200,134	100,389	99,745

Note: Figures assume 25% income tax bracket with contributions made at beginning of year.

An individual in the 25% income tax bracket who annually contributes $1,500 to an 8% IRA tax-sheltered plan (compounded daily for an effective yield of 8.45%) will reap nearly $100,000 more after 30 years than if he were to place the equivalent money in a non-sheltered account.

• *Keogh plans.* Under a regular Keogh plan, a self-employed individual can shelter 15% of earned income up to a maximum of $7,500 a year. However, under new liberalized regulations, a self-employed person can now set up a *defined benefit (super) Keogh plan*, which allows the person to decide the annual income he or she wants and the number of years he or she wants it. The amount an individual will be able to get depends on age when the plan is set up, current income, and the number of years until retirement. Under the actuarial formula set up by law, at present $50,000 is generally the most income that can be used to formulate a plan, and the percentage of income ranges from 6.5% at age 30 or less to 2% at age 60 or more. A good actuary can figure it out for you; contact your nearest commercial bank or insurance company.

Some trustees now allow IRA and Keogh plans to be set up using gold coins, stamps, and diamonds as investments. To set up such a plan, you'd either have to convince the trustee of your present plan to go along or find one who will set up such an "exotic" program. You can find a list of such trustees from:

• Gem Hedge International, 440 Park Ave. S., New York, NY 10016 (diamonds)
• Scott Publishing Co., 3 East 57th St., New York, NY 10022 (stamps)
• Deak-Perera, 1800 K St. N.W., Washington, DC 20006 (rare coins)

Remember: you will pay a penalty if you withdraw prematurely (before age 59½) from such plans, but you must start to withdraw by age 70½.

Anyone for Annuities?

Annuities are contracts sold by insurance companies that guarantee you a fixed payment for life (and sometimes to a beneficiary after you die) of a fixed number of dollars each month. The typical annuity purchaser is near retirement, lacks a big capital fund but does have some assets, doesn't like to take risks, and wants to be free of money-management chores. Above all, he's in good health and stands a fair chance of beating the mortality tables, thereby collecting more annuity payments than usual.

You can buy several types of annuities, either in a lump sum or in installments. Annuities have some tax advantages because taxes are deferred on interest built up until you actually get the interest in annuity payments. And the payout that represents return of capital is usually tax exempt. However, because of the relatively low interest buildup, it usually doesn't pay to begin payments earlier than age 55—the longer you wait to start collecting benefits, the better. While a man of 65 might draw out around $7 per $1,000 of straight life annuity per month, this sum rises to around $9 per month at age 70.

If you want to guarantee payments for a certain number of years for yourself and/or a dependent, get a *life annuity with installments certain*. You could also buy a *cash refund* annuity that pays your beneficiary a lump sum if you die before collecting the original investment. If you have little or no life insurance, you might consider a *joint and survivor annuity*. This works best if you and your spouse are around the same age or state of health; if one is younger, the payments might be too low.

Here's what you might get in monthly annuity income for every $1,000.

Type of Annuity	Monthly Income
Straight life	$6.75
Life income—10 yrs. certain	6.16
Life income—20 yrs. certain	4.94
Life income—installment refund	5.57
Joint and survivor (two-thirds to survivor)	5.72

If you're middle-aged (over age 45), earning more than $30,000 a year, with a good-sized savings account, home almost paid for, and few financial obligations, look into a *variable annuity*. In a variable annuity, the insurance company invests your premiums in common and preferred stocks. You build up "units" that will pay you a monthly income. However, the company usually deducts a 15% sales charge the first year and a 7% charge each subsequent year, so your payments aren't fully invested in the portfolio. If the portfolio increases in value, you'll get fatter checks, varying with the swing of the market. You pay taxes only on the investment gains portion of your monthly payments.

You choose the usual payout plans described earlier, but the number of units you receive each month differs with the type of payout plan. You can cancel the plan before payment starts and get back whatever your value is in the fund or borrow against this value. Or you can switch your units back and forth between a variable and a fixed annuity—valuable if you're able to predict the stock market's ups and downs. However, over the past years, variable annuities have been only second best to savings accounts.

If you're over age 54, have good capital gains on securities, want to avoid capital gains tax, and don't mind invading capital, look into *charitable annuities*. In many cases you can buy these annuities with appreciated securities, paying little or no tax. Other tax credits and advantages include an income tax credit corresponding to your life expectancy for your contribution to a nonprofit organization (charitable tax deduction). With charitable annuities you are assured an income for life, or you may select a contract with installments.

For information on charitable annuities, check your favorite nonprofit service, charitable, religious, or educational organization, including the Red Cross, Salvation Army, American Heart Association, American Bible Society, etc. Other annuities include *increasing* (3% compounded annually as long as policy is in effect) and *investment* (you retain investment management of assets).

It pays to shop around for an annuity. When stock and bond markets are strong, insurance companies usually cut annuity prices. In many cases there's a wide gap (perhaps 20%) in the prices between the least and most expensive annuity paying the same benefits.

Annuities aren't for everyone. People in the middle years can profit more by investing in tax-exempt bonds and buy an annuity later on. If you're interested in annuities at all, at least combine the variable annuity with a fixed one.

Some companies specializing in annuities are:

- First Investment Annuity of America, Valley Forge Executive Mall, P.O. Box 831, Valley Forge, PA 19482
- Anchor National Life Insurance, Anchor National Life Plaza, Camelback at 22nd St., Phoenix, AZ 85016
- Phoenix Mutual Life, One American Row, Hartford, CT 06115

- Capital Life, 1600 Sherman St., Denver, CO 80201
- Life Insurance of Georgia, 600 W. Peachtree St. NW, Atlanta, GA 30308

Besides *home ownership* (mortgage interest and property taxes) and *trusts* (income can go to a nontaxpaying beneficiary) you have other alternatives:

- *Single-premium deferred annuities.* Generally, you pay a single premium (usually $10,000) about 10 years before retirement, and the money earns interest (from about 3½ to 7%) tax free until you start withdrawing it on a regularly monthly basis for the rest of your life. Many brokerage houses are now selling these annuities and you can buy them directly from such companies as:

- Aetna Life
- American General
- Anchor National
- Bankers National
- Kansas City Life
- Life & Casualty

Contact local agents or brokers for further information.

- *Realty partnerships, cattle plans, oil and gas development drilling programs.* If you're in the top income brackets and have a minimum of $5,000 to $10,000 to invest, you can tax shelter in these plans. However, *all involve risk* and should be entered into only with the advice of a lawyer (who can check the soundness of the deal and the reputation of the management) and an *accountant* (who can check the income and expense projections and possible tax advantages). Some programs are sold publicly and can be bought through brokerage houses. But deal only with the most reliable houses, and be sure of any possible tax liabilities as well as tax advantages.

What About Some Other Tax Shelters?

How To Make Money In Collectibles

Paintings, drawings, prints, antiques, Chinese ceramics, rare coins, diamonds, books, letters, autographs, stamps—all can serve as excellent investment vehicles. But you must know what to buy and how to buy. Here are some of the ground rules for success.

When leading banks, brokerage houses, and the U.S. Department of Labor agree—it's got to be right. They all agree that *collectibles*—everything from art to wine jars—can belong (about 20% of total) in a "prudent man's" investment portfolio.

The following figures bear out the facts. Over a 10-year period (1969–79) here is the compounded annual rate of return on various investments as measured by Salomon Brothers, investment banking firm:

Investment	Compounded Annual Rate of Return
Chinese ceramics	18.0%
Rare books	16.5%
Gold	16.3%
Stamps	15.4%
Coins	13.0%
Oil (crude, at the wellhead)	11.8%
Paintings (old masters)	11.6%
Farmland	10.6%
Housing	9.2%
Consumer Price Index	*6.1%*
Bonds	6.1%
Stocks	2.9%

As you can see, it would pay you to investigate the profits and pleasures in collectibles. Here are some tips on getting started:

1. *Specialize in a field of interest or expertise.* You should have some personal or professional interest in your field—perhaps some area related to your job or hobby. A pharmacist might collect old apothecary equipment; a publisher, rare books; a photographer, old cameras and photographs.

2. *Buy what you like.* Amateurs who buy with the hope of selling quickly at a profit are usually disappointed. But if you buy something you personally enjoy, you'll at least get some pleasure out of the item if not profit. Also, try to avoid fads that can quickly change. And shy away from items that can be easily faked or copied. It would help if your collectible had a *collector's club* or a trade paper devoted to the subject. Also, try to concentrate on items that will form a collection; the whole will be worth more than individual pieces.

3. *Expand your knowledge.* Read books and magazines in your field, attend auctions, exhibits, collector's club meetings, contact museum curators and appraisers. Some good books for beginners are:

- *Investments You Can Live With and Enjoy* by Richard H. Rush (U.S. News Books)
- *The Insiders Guide to Antiques, Art, & Collectibles* by Sylvia O'Neil Dorn (Cornerstone Library)
- *Investing for Pleasure and Profit* by John Peterson (Dow Jones Books)
- *The Time-Life Encyclopedia of Collectibles*, a series of volumes (Time-Life Books)

4. *Get to know your dealer.* A good dealer will recommend reading materials and exhibits, give written guarantees, allow independent appraisals and would permit collectors to exchange items or trade them in. Preferably, the dealer should be a member of a professional society and a member of the Better Business Bureau or Chamber of Commerce. At least, call the local Better Business Bureau or similar organization to see if the dealer is registered and if there have been any problems or complaints. For national organizations, contact the Council of Better Business Bureaus, 1150 17th St. NW, Washington, DC 20036.

5. *Get independent appraisals.* Besides many independent testing laboratories, you can sometimes get appraisals at local museums, universities, and galleries. You can also contact the American Society of Appraisers, 60 E. 42nd St., New York, NY 10017 and the Appraisers Association of America, 541 Lexington Ave., New York, NY 10022 for members near you.

6. *Get a certificate of authenticity.* Many professional societies offer certification services. As was mentioned earlier, you should get a "dealer's certificate of title, guarantee of genuineness, and registration" or *at least* a written guarantee (on the sales slip) of authenticity, specifying the artist's name and the work's date, title, medium, previous ownership or whatever else is important.

7. *Know the price and expect to pay a reasonable sum.* Price guides are available for most collectibles, and/or you can get publications from your local library (like *Art Investment Report*) that will give you ideas of current prices. Expect to pay what the item is worth, but don't be afraid to ask if there's a discount. However, if the item is marked "50% off" or if the dealer offers a big discount on a marked item, it was either overpriced to being with or the dealer isn't sure of its true worth. To check prices, look on your newsstand for *Price Guide to Antiques and Collectibles*, published quarterly by Babka Publishing Co., 100 Bryant St., Dubuque, IA 52001.

8. *Set up a budget and stick to quality.* Determine how much you can afford to invest during a year (about 20% of investment capital is tops) and put limits on any one purchase. But stick to quality: one

$1,000 investment in the work of a famous artist is worth more than $100 each in 10 obscure works. If you can't afford a master's top-quality painting, specialize in his less expensive drawings and prints. Also, *have enough cash reserve.* You might find it hard to sell an object on short notice. In fact, most experts advise that *you might have to wait 10 years* to realize a worthwhile gain on your collectible.

9. *Investigate the resale market.* If the dealer or seller offers to "buy back" the item, get it in writing. Also know what other markets are available: auctions, flea markets, dealers in the field, specialty publications (see "How to Sell Collectibles" section at the end of this chapter).

10. *Know the tax angles.* If you collect as an *investor,* you can write off expenses to the amount of income produced by a sale. And you can write off losses from sales. But you may have to limit the personal use of your purchases and, if you're a dealer, be able to show a profit for at least two years out of five. We'll discuss this in greater detail in the "How to Sell" section.

If 20 years ago you had bought some old masters' prints (limited editions of original works) by such masters as Dürer, Rembrandt, Goya, Hals, Ruisdael, Toulouse-Lautrec, Matisse, Pissarro, Picasso, or Utrillo, *your investment would have multiplied 40 times by now.* Other art categories would also show substantial gains: modern up 30 times; old masters' drawings, 25 times; impressionists, 20 times; English, 12 times; old masters' paintings, 10 times.

The Art of Investing in Art

What makes art a valuable investment? Experts say that a painting or print should be of recognized artistic quality, rare (including limited editions of etchings, engravings, and lithographs), in *good original condition,* of proved authenticity, and have historical appeal. One fine print might be worth $25,000; a poor impression of the same print in poor condition may be worth less than $1,000.

In recent years demand for collecting and investing has been strong for the works of the old masters; nineteenth-century Continental, British, and American artists; twentieth-century American realists and abstract artists; international abstract expressionists and surrealists; postimpressionists and French Moderns; eighteenth-century British artists; and the American painters Russell and Remington.

If you can't afford an original oil or watercolor, consider buying drawings and prints. A master's painting may cost $100,000, but his drawings (pencil, ink, charcoal, crayon) may cost $10,000 and his prints (reproductions from etchings, engravings, woodcuts, lithographs), about $1,000. The biggest names command the most, with Rembrandt, Dürer, Canaletti, Picasso, Toulouse-Lautrec, and Whistler drawing top dollar. But for around $100 you can still invest in prints by Goya, Daumier, Innes, or Collot. Get drawings or prints in good condition, preferably those with signatures.

For further information:

- *A Guide to the Collecting and Care of Original Prints* by Carl Zigrosser and Christa M. Gaehde (Crown)
- *Practical Guide to Print Collecting* by Ann Buchsbaum (Van Nostrand)
- *Fine Prints: Collecting, Buying, Selling* by Cecile Shapiro and Lauris Mason (Harper & Row)

Before buying art for investment, learn as much as possible by attending seminars, frequenting galleries, and perhaps taking a course in art history. And heed this advice from art dealer John Richardson of M. Knoedler & Co.: "For people who buy art out of an obsession—true collectors—art usually turns out to be a good investment. Whereas people who buy primarily as an investment nearly always end up losing money."

Jumping Profits from Antiques Antiques are artistic objects (generally furniture but also glass, toys, musical instruments, jewelry, medals, pictures, etc.) usually over 100 years old. Among favorites are European furniture and other objects, Victorian pieces, and early American antiques. Recent best buys include eighteenth and nineteenth-century Early American furniture, Georgian silver, American silver of early to middle nineteenth century, French carpets, eighteenth-century Dutch furniture, Oriental antiques (including Japanese *netsuke*), Italian furniture, Delft china, and French and English bronzes.

You can also make sound investments in furniture by Chippendale, Sheraton, Phyfe, Alden, Carver, Brewster, and Benjamin Franklin. (Franklin supposedly invented the rocking chair as well as a fan chair.) If your pieces are associated with important events or persons, you'll have a rarer treasure. Chairs of the Louis XIV, XV, and XVI periods, for example, command regal prices.

But for much lower prices you can buy early American furniture that would be pleasurable to behold and profitable to possess. Among the most popular groups:

- *Federal furniture* (1790 to 1850). Top American craftsmen—the Seymours, Duncan Phyfe, Shaw, Connelly—derived most of their designs from George Hepplewhite and Thomas Sheraton, the English cabinetmakers. Best buys are small chairs, loveseats, card tables, and sidetables.
- *Empire furniture* (1815 to 1835). Duncan Phyfe is still the big

name here, with Lannulier in second place among American cabinet-makers. Matched pairs are especially profitable.

• *Victorian furniture* (1835 to 1900). Much of this furniture is wildly ornate, but lighter and simpler pieces were made by Henry Belter. They sell from about $300 to $2,500.

• *Country or "Primitive"* (1800 to 1900). This is simple, utilitarian furniture sold in most antique shops. The best pieces were made before 1870 and are sturdy and graceful without frills. Especially good buys are bentwood chairs and trestle tables.

While you can get good antique buys through dealers and antique stores, you could save the 50 to 100% dealer markup by buying at auction. The famous houses of *Sotheby Parke Bernet* (980 Madison Ave., New York, NY 10021) and *Christie's* (502 Park Ave., New York, NY 10022) hold regular auctions in various parts of the country. Write for details.

If you buy through a dealer, your best bet would be a member of the National Antique & Art Dealers Association (122 E. 57th St., New York, NY 10022) or the Art Dealers Association of America (575 Madison Ave., New York NY 10022). You can also follow publications specializing in antiques, including:

• *American Art & Antiques*, 1515 Broadway, New York, NY 10036
• *Antiques*, 551 Fifth Ave., New York, NY 10017
• *Antique Monthly*, Boone, Inc., Drawer 2, Tuscaloosa, AL 35401

Also ask your librarian for some of these books:

• *The Collector's Complete Directory of American Antiques* by Frances Phipps (Doubleday)
• *American Heritage History of American Antiques* (Simon & Schuster)
• *The Impecunious Collector's Guide to American Antiques* by John Kirk (Knopf)

Antiques don't have to be confined to the rare and expensive—or even objects over 100 years old. Investors today make money investing modest sums in weather vanes, "action" banks, glass of all kinds, wind-up Victrolas, Currier and Ives prints, violin bows, cameo brooches, barometers, globes, figureheads, guns, armor, religious objects, clocks, spoons, etc.

For articles and advertisements of buying and selling opportunities in antiques, sent 50 cents for a sample copy of *The American Collector's Journal*, P.O. Box 1431, Porterville, CA 93258.

The Special Appeal of Chinese Ceramics

As you saw at the start of this chapter, Chinese ceramics have appreciated more in value than any other collectible. Not only are they the most profitable; they are among the most pleasing possessions. Here are some tips on ceramic investing:

Periods and Pieces

The following have proved most profitable and popular through the years:

- *Han* (206 BC to 220 AD). These pieces are very primitive, natural in color, and not highly decorated. Some green-glazed Han items recently sold for $2,500 and up.
- *T'ang* (618 AD to 907 AD). These pieces aren't extremely rare and are generally more decorative than the Han pieces. Some of them recently have been going for around $2,000 and up.
- *Sung* (960 AD to 1280 AD). These include simple but very decorative figures like wine jars, bowls, and vases. Prices range from about $1,000.
- *Ming* (1368 AD to 1644 AD). Generally rather ornate and decorative in a sophisticated manner, they include dishes, bowls, and vases. Prices range from as low as $350 to as high as $250,000.

Value

Rarity and condition determine value. The less rare the piece, the more damage can diminish its value. A very rare red underglaze Ming piece can have more damage with less adverse effect on price than a blue underglaze piece. The hardest job for the novice is to separate the genuine from copies and fakes. However, most period pieces have a characteristic "crackle"—a network of fine cracks on the surface. After you've learned the characteristic crackle of a period, you should examine the piece with a high-powered magnifying glass to make sure that it is genuine. For example, there's generally much more crackle on a genuine T'ang piece than on fakes. Museums may be able to give you more definitive judgments, or you can send color photos of ceramics to auction houses like Sotheby Parke Bernet or Christie's and they may be able to give you an estimate of true worth.

These books give further information:

- *A Connoisseur's Guide to Chinese Ceramics* by Cecile and Michel Beurdeley (Harper & Row)
- *Collecting Chinese Export Porcelain* by Elinor Gordon (Universe)
- *Chinese Export Porcelain: An Historical Survey* (Universe)

As Leonard Sime, publisher of the *American Collector's Journal* says: "The more you know, the luckier your get." This holds especially true in Chinese ceramics.

Besides the gold and silver coins mentioned earlier, other rare coins have appreciated over the last 10 years at an annual rate of 13%.

Some Coins Are Better Than Cash

You're probably best off with rare U.S. coins for these reasons: (1) they aren't as easily faked as some foreign coins; (2) there's always a ready market here; (3) they can't be worth less than face value; (4) good selective coins have averaged 30% and more in value over the years.

Some good rare U.S. coin buys are:

- Indian head and Lincoln cents (especially early dates—1909, 1914)
- Buffalo and Jefferson nickels (uncirculated and proof Jeffersons)
- Standing Liberty and Washington quarters (1916 to 1930)
- Standing Liberty and uncirculated Franklin half dollars
- Silver dollars through 1935
- $1 gold pieces (in the best condition)
- $20 Saint-Gauden gold pieces

Once you've decided what to collect, start with coins that have the best condition. A coin meant for general circulation—not a proof—that has absolutely no wear is known as an *uncirculated coin*.

Several good books show how to determine the condition based on wear. Among these books are:

- *A Guide Book of United States Coins* by R. S. Yeoman (Western Publishing)
- *Collecting Rare Coins for Profit* by David Bowers (Harper & Row)
- *The World of Coins* (Hodder and Stoughton)

You could also contact these organizations for information:

- American Numismatic Association, P.O. Box 2366, Colorado Springs, CO 80901
- American Numismatic Society, 617 West 155th St., New York, NY 10032

And these periodicals would be helpful (available at libraries):

- *Coin World*, 911 Vandemark Rd., Sidney, OH 45365
- *Numismatic News*, Krause Publications, 700 E. State St., Iola, WI 54995

When buying coins, deal through reputable local dealers. Be sure to get a bill of sale or a certificate that states the coin's genuineness. Avoid mail-order dealers who may "guarantee" you a 10% or better return on any investment; no one can make such a guarantee.

Diamonds May (or May Not) Be Your Best Investment

Although some diamonds have appreciated 25 to 30% a year, *prices may now be too high.* Speculative fever has driven the price of a fine carat as high as $30,000 with no end in sight. Besides that, the dealer markup on diamonds is easily 20 to 100%. It might take you 3 to 5 good years to make up the difference in this spread just to break even.

Generally, the larger the stone, the more valuable and the greater the rate of appreciation. Many experts feel that a *two carat* diamond is minimum investment grade. However, the average stone now is about ¾ carats, and many dealers feel that the average-size 5 years from now will be ½ carat. And some experts feel that *baguettes*—very small diamonds used in jewelry settings—can be a good investment. However, figure you're going to need *at least $5,000* to invest in diamonds.

If you invest, you should concentrate on gems certified as D through J on the *color* scale. Color accounts for about 50% of value; 25% might go to *clarity*, which should be flawless through VS1. And in terms of *cut* or shape, only the round brilliant stone is generally accepted.

There's an old saying in the diamond industry that's worth repeating: "If you don't know your diamonds, know who you're dealing with." There are many shady operators in this field, and you're entirely at the mercy of the dealer. If in doubt, check the dealer out with the Better Business Bureau. And the stone *must* be certified by a leading grading house like *The Gemological Institute.* This organization gives *quality gradings* on loose stones, and they offer courses on diamond appraising and helpful literature for sale. You may contact GIA at:

580 Fifth Ave.   1660 Stewart St.
New York, NY 10036   Santa Monica, CA 90404

Before considering investing in diamonds, you should read up on the subject. Some good books (usually available at libraries) are:

- *Gemstones* by G. F. Smith (Pitman Publishers)
- *Gems* by Robert Webster (Shoe String Press)
- *Gemstones of North America* by John Sinkankas (Van Nostrand)
- *Practical Gemmology and Gemmoligist Compendium* by Robert Webster (Gamzon Bros.)

You should also consider subscribing to the leading journal in the field:

The Lapidary Journal, P.O. Box 80937, San Diego, CA 92138.

And remember—this warning appeared not too long ago in an advertisement placed by Tiffany's, New York's leading jeweler: ". . . some speculators have driven diamond prices too high. We suggest you *look before you leap.*"

Profits and Pleasures in Literary Collectibles

Literary collectibles—books, atlases, letters, maps, autographs—have appreciated 10 to 50% annually over the past 5 years. The "thrill of the chase" (you can find these items in the most unexpected places like attics or flea markets) makes literary collectibles almost as popular as coins and stamps. And you can generally buy these items for prices ranging from $10 to $100 (and up), making literary collectibles less expensive than art works or antiques.

To get started, pick a field of interest (subject) or specialize in an author or famous person. A doctor might specialize in treatises in his medical specialty; a singer in manuscripts of her best-loved composer; a traveler in maps of his or her favorite country. Some popular and profitable fields include sports, medical and scientific, works of great and classic authors, Americana (before 1880), limited editions of modern American authors, and maps and atlases. Signed letters, books, manuscripts of the famous and infamous are sought after for autographs. Whatever your specialty, remember that *a collection is worth more than the sum of its parts.* You can sometimes sell a collection costing from $2,000 to $5,000 for as much as $10,000 to college, public, and museum libraries (or donate the collection for a tax deduction).

A rare combination might be a first edition, even first and second printings from original plates of a book, atlas, or map . . . or an original letter or manuscript "dedicated" or presented to the recipient (the author signs his name and the name of the person to whom he gave the document). To focus on a subject or author, look up *bibliographies* in the card catalog of your local library. Your reference librarian may know several relevant reference works and probably has a copy of the *World Bibliography of Bibliographies.* If your library has a rare books' division, start there to learn about the field.

The next step is to locate a reliable dealer. You can sometimes find literary collectibles by browsing in flea markets, garage sales, second-hand bookstores; in old chests, trunks, and boxes in your attic. But a specialist will be a more dependable source, as well as someone who can help you evaluate your "finds." You can locate the names of dealers in your area by consulting at your library: *Book Dealers in North America, AB Bookman's Weekly, The Book Collector.* You can also get a list of member-dealers of the Antiquarian Booksellers Center by sending a self-addressed business-sized stamped envelope to the Center at 50 Rockefeller Plaza, New York, NY 10020.

Whatever author, subject, or document you specialize in, get the *best available copy*. A book in "mint" condition would have original bindings (not rebound) and a clean dust jacket; would not be a library copy showing markings; would not be stained, moldy, or with loose or missing pages. The five magic words in the antique document business are: *age, rarity, quality, condition*, and *fashion*.

Expect to pay what the literary collectible is worth. You can check prices in *American Book Prices Current* by Kathy and Van Leab and other books found in most major libraries. If you sell a book or document, most dealers will give you *only half* the price they think they'll be able to get. You might get a better price by contacting an auction house or contact a specialist, a dealer who trades in your particular field, located through the sources above. And, as with any collectible, buy for your pleasure as well as for any profit you hope to make. For further information:

- *New Gold in Your Attic* and *The Book Collectors Handbook* by Van Allen Bradley
- *ABC for Book Collectors* by John Carter
- *Book Collecting as a Hobby* by Percy H. Muir Randall
- *Collecting Autographs and Manuscripts* by Charles Hamilton
- *Autographs: A Collector's Guide* by Jerry E. Patterson

Stamps That Hedge Against Inflation

Top-quality postage stamps have been appreciating at about 30%, and the trend is expected to continue for the next couple of years or more.

How do you get started? The beginner should study carefully, pick a specialized field of collecting (perhaps something related to a business or interest), know what he's doing before buying, and start small with good-quality stamps ($50 to $500). A stamp's value depends upon *scarcity, topic, design appeal*, and *country of issue*. On a quality scale denoting the degree of centering of the image or design, the gradations are "superb," "very fine," "good," and "fair." A stamp in mint condition will have the original gum back, and it will be well-centered, with complete perforations on all sides. Tears, repairs, faded colors, and hinges reduce the investment quality of the stamp. Your best bet is to *buy only "superb" or "very fine" stamps*.

The best investment opportunities might lie in stamps issued before 1900 or higher-priced stamps issued up to 1930 by those countries that print a wide variety of a limited number of stamps each year: U.S., Great Britain and the Commonwealth, Germany, France, Italy, Switzerland, Japan, and Scandinavia. Countries that are or have been in the news recently also have appeal: Israel, Egypt, Thailand, etc. U.S.

commemoratives issued before 1920 are also good buys, and the "classics" are U.S. issues of 1847 through 1900 and British issues of 1840 to 1900.

Also good investments are Graf Zeppelin airmails issued in 1930, which have increased in value about 30% a year; and $5 Columbians, which have appreciated at an annual rate of about 16%. You can get help from members of the American Stamp Dealers Association, 595 Madison Ave., New York, NY 10022.

Some stamps have been faked, and other have been inflated in established reputable dealers. If in doubt, arrange to have stamps authenticated by the American Philatelic Society, P.O. Box 800, State College, PA 16801. Write to them for details. A similar service is offered by the Philatelic Foundation, 270 Madison Ave., New York, NY 10016. And note that the Federal Trade Commission has recently ruled that sending stamps "on approval" without a customer's permission is illegal.

If buying at auction, stick to major houses like Sotheby Parke Bernet (980 Madison Ave., New York, NY 10021) or B. D. Harmer (6 West 48th St., New York, NY 10036). Such auctions are also excellent places to learn about current price trends.

You *should* study the philatelic market like you do the stock market. To do so, see if your library or bookstore has one or more of the following books:

- *Stamps for Investment* by Kenneth R. Lake (Stein & Day)
- *Fun and Profit in Stamp Collecting* by Herman Herst (Philatelic Book Pub.)
- *A Guide to Stamp Collecting* (Minkus Publications)
- *The New York Times Guide to Collecting Stamps* by David Lidman
- *Standard Handbook of Stamp Collecting* by Richard McB. Cabeen (Thomas Y, Crowell Co.)

You can also subscribe to these publications (write for subscription details):

- *Linn's Stamp News*, P.O. Box 150, Sidney, OH 45365
- *The Stamp Market Report*, P.O. Box 1328, Jackson, NJ 08527

And for information on stamp catalogs and prices and a copy of *Stamp Market Update,* a quarterly newsletter on current trends and prices in the philatelic marketplace, write: *Scott*, 3 E. 57th St., New York, NY 10022

Now's the Time to Also Consider Selling Some Collectibles

During a recession, the prices of many collectibles—except those that are truly rare and valuable—often drop in price. This presents both *buying* opportunities (when prices are lowest) and *selling* opportunities (before prices sink too low).

By selling (or making an attempt to do so), you can convince the Internal Revenue Service that you are an *investor* rather than just a collector. A collector buys merely for pleasure; an investor mainly for profit (although you can still get limited use and enjoyment from the items).

As an investor, you can claim certain tax advantages: (1) travel to acquire or sell items; (2) expenses in advertising and displaying the item for sale; (3) sales commissions to auction houses; and (4) other selling expenses. You could write off any *losses* made on a sale, and you'd be taxed at favorable capital-gains rates if you held the item for a year or longer. And as an investor, you can write off expenses associated with holding the asset against other income in the year you incur them.

In some instances you can make money by *donating* your collectibles to a museum. This could be especially profitable on items that have greatly appreciated in value (The IRS would want an appraiser's report).

Perhaps the first question you should ask yourself is, "What makes the collection valuable?" Here are some reasons:

- age
- beauty
- color
- fashion
- historical interest
- materials
- period and style
- quality
- rarity
- source and originality
- subject
- workmanship

The next question to ask is, "Who would want the item and why?" Perhaps it might be a *museum* or *educational institution* because of its relevance to certain other collections or subject matter; perhaps to *dealers* who specialize in the item or who are recognized experts in the field; to *individuals* who might be interested for sentimental, ethnic, religious, or other reasons; to *corporations* or *associations* which might want your collectible because it fits into their product line, membership interest, or research activities.

And perhaps most important is "How much is the item worth?" While most investment collectibles have risen in price at least 10 to 15% annually, you may not be exactly aware of their current value. However, as noted earlier, there are price guides available for most collectibles.

Leading auction houses like Sotheby Parke Bernet (980 Madison Ave., New York, NY 10021) and *Christie's* (502 Park Ave., New York, NY 10022) will sometimes give an informal appraisal free if you send in a photograph. However, for valuable items they will charge a fee based on the value of the collection and time spent. This could range from $500 to $1,000 per appraiser per day. Less expensive might be members of the *American Society of Appraisers* (60 East 42nd St., New York, NY 10017) and the Appraisers Association of America (541 Lexington Ave., New York, NY 10022) which might charge $50 to $125 per hour or a percentage of the appraised value.

Once you've determined an item's true value, add in all acquiring and selling costs (see below) and *price the item to sell*—probably at no more than 10% above total costs and value. (If it has appreciated in value, you've already made a good profit.)

Then, depending upon your time, degree of expertise, and value of your collectible, here are some major selling outlets to consider:

1. *Advertising in publications*. It's often been said that the more precisely you can describe your item, the faster you can sell it at a good price. A *detailed* and *clear* classified ad in publications like *The American Collector's Journal* (P.O. Box 1431, Porterville, CA 93258) can bring immediate results. A display ad—with photo—will bring even better results. Picture the item head on or straight down with minimum of space distortion, plus a measurement (such as a ruler) to show size. Use black backgrounds for clear glass, contrasting backgrounds for other items. *State price* unless you want to request bids or start a correspondence that could lead to a sale. Use a box number if the item is valuable.

2. *Direct mail*. If you can target your audience to members of an organization (collectors' clubs or associations), you can sell your item with a personal letter, including a photo. You can find addresses of such organizations from *Encyclopedia of Associations* (Gale Research Co.) available at or through most libraries. Write directly to the club to see if you can rent or buy their lists or go through a list broker (see telephone directory) specializing in such organizations.

3. *Rummage, garage, and yard sales*. For less valuable items, you can set up a table or stand in a neighborhood parking lot, empty store, back of fire or police station, a garage, or yard. Put price tags on all items and have plenty of bags on hand to package the items.

4. *"Flea markets."* For $10 to $25 you can rent space at markets that are often held in public places such as state fairgrounds. The market usually does general advertising for you, and you can be assured of a good crowd.

5. *Antique and craft shows*. These are sponsored by civic or charitable organizations and held in quality hotels, motels, houses of

worship, etc. You pay $10 to $50 for space, and usually the shows are widely advertised and publicized in local papers, newsletters, and specialty publications that reach dealers as well as specialized investors. *The American Crafts Council*, 44 W. 53th St., New York, NY 10019 has publications and other information that is helpful in selling crafts.

6. *Auctions*. The top auction houses charge 10% to seller and 10% to buyer, while regional houses (Robert Skinner in Boston, Morton's in New Orleans, Milwaukee Galleries, Butterfield & Butterfield in San Francisco) may charge 20 to 25% to the seller. Established auction houses are honest (you can always check with the Better Business Bureau), but you should get all terms in writing, including commissions, advertising fees, minimum bids, additional charges for storing, insurance, and moving, date of sale, and date of payment (usually one week after sale). Remember, *sales commissions are negotiable*, especially if you have a major piece. But don't be afraid to sell minor pieces at an auction; most auction sales are for under $1,000.

7. *Dealers*. This is an excellent place to raise quick money, but you'll probably get only half the retail price. Your best bet might be the dealer you bought the item from or members of the *National Antique and Art Dealers Association* (122 E. 57th St., New York, NY 10022), *Art Dealers Association of America* (575 Madison Ave., New York, NY 10022), or similar professional associations. Dealers are prime prospects for collections or collectibles worth $3,000 or more—especially specialized or unique items. *Try to get the dealer to make the first offer.* If you must set the price, state it higher than you expect to get, but not ridiculously so (40% more would be tops). Be prepared to split the difference between his offer and yours. It helps if you're well dressed and can drop a name or two associated with the item or collection. In some cases you can get a better price by letting the dealer sell on *consignment*. Fees run from 10 to 30% of the item (vs. the 40 to 50% you'd sacrifice on a direct sale). Set a *time limit* for any consignment sale, usually three to six months. If it doesn't sell, you can then have it auctioned. You can locate dealers by looking in the telephone book under "bought and sold" for the particular item. Ask if they take items on consignment.

Besides the books, publications, and associations mentioned earlier, here are some good books on the subject. Most should be available at or through your local library:

- *How to Sell Your Collectibles, Antiques & Crafts at a Profit* by Marguerite Ashworth Brunner (Rawson Associates)
- *The Insiders Guide to Antiques, Art, & Collectibles* by Sylvia O'Neill Dorn (Cornerstone Library)

- *Where to Sell It Directory* (available from Pilot Books, 347 Fifth Ave., New York, NY 10016).

You could also write these publications for subscription information:

- *Collectibles Monthly*, Box 2023, York, PA 17405
- *Covels on Antiques and Collectibles*, Beachwood, OH 44122

Remember, "The more you know, the luckier you get."

How To Make Money On Savings Accounts

Passbook rates have been so dwarfed by inflation that having "money in the bank" is no longer the goal of ambitious people. But you still need savings to cover emergencies. Here's how to maximize the yield you receive on "rainy day" money.

You need savings to cover emergencies and to protect your other investments. Some financial experts say you should have 3 to 6 months' living expenses in savings. However, you can raise or lower this amount according to your income security, health and other insurance, defensive and aggressive investments, and plans for the future. But *at least 3 months' expenses* provides a sound financial foundation.

Where do you put the money? As you'll see, you have several choices. Each has advantages and disadvantages. The following questions are a good place to start:

- *What services do you want?* Commercial banks offer the most services, including all types of loans, rental of safety deposit boxes, investment advice and fulfillment, sale of travelers checks, and even payment of utility bills. Other savings institutions offer fewer services—just make sure they offer the ones you need and want.
- *How is interest compounded?* Some financial institutions com-

Year	4.50%	5.00%	5.50%	6.00%	6.50%	7.00%	8.00%	9.00%	10.00%
1	$104.50	$105.00	$105.50	$106.00	$106.50	$107.00	$108.00	$109.00	$ 110.00
2	109.20	110.25	111.30	112.36	113.42	114.49	116.64	118.81	121.00
3	114.12	115.76	117.42	119.10	120.80	122.50	125.97	129.50	133.10
4	119.25	121.55	123.88	126.25	128.65	131.08	136.05	141.16	146.41
5	124.62	127.63	130.70	133.82	137.01	140.26	146.93	153.86	161.05
6	130.23	134.01	137.88	141.85	145.91	150.07	158.69	167.71	177.16
7	136.09	140.71	145.47	150.36	155.40	160.58	171.38	182.80	194.87
8	142.21	147.75	153.47	159.38	165.50	171.82	185.09	199.26	214.36
9	148.61	155.13	161.91	168.95	176.26	183.85	199.90	217.19	235.79
10	155.30	162.89	170.81	179.08	187.71	196.72	215.89	236.74	259.37
11	162.29	171.03	180.21	189.83	199.92	210.49	233.16	258.04	285.31
12	169.59	179.59	190.12	201.22	212.91	225.22	251.82	281.27	313.84
13	177.22	188.56	200.58	213.29	226.75	240.98	271.96	306.58	345.23
14	185.19	197.99	211.61	226.09	241.49	257.85	293.72	334.17	379.75
15	193.53	207.89	223.25	239.66	257.18	275.90	317.22	364.25	417.72
16	202.24	218.29	235.53	254.04	273.90	295.22	342.59	397.03	459.50
17	211.34	229.20	248.48	269.28	291.70	315.88	370.00	432.76	505.45
18	220.85	240.66	262.15	285.43	310.67	337.99	399.60	471.71	555.99
19	230.79	252.70	276.56	302.56	330.86	361.65	431.57	514.17	611.59
20	241.17	265.33	291.78	320.71	352.36	386.97	466.10	560.44	672.75
21	252.02	278.60	307.82	339.96	375.27	414.06	503.38	610.08	740.03
22	263.37	292.53	324.75	360.35	399.66	443.04	543.65	665.86	814.03
23	275.22	307.15	342.62	381.98	425.64	474.05	587.15	725.79	895.43
24	287.60	322.51	361.46	404.89	453.31	507.24	634.12	791.11	984.97
25	300.54	338.64	381.34	429.19	482.77	542.74	684.85	862.31	1083.47

Over the long term, seemingly modest differences in the rate at which interest is compounded can lead to enormous differences in the amount of money you will have. Look at what $100 turns into after 25 yeats at 4.50%, at 5.50% at 6.50%, at 8.00%, and at 10.00%!

pute interest on the "low balance method"—you receive interest only for the lowest balance in your account. Others offer "day of deposit to day of withdrawal," in which you receive pro-rated interest credit for any money you put into the account, regardless of how long you leave it there. Still others offer "grace" or "bonus" days in which you earn interest on money you haven't yet deposited. For instance, any money you deposit during the first 10 days of each quarter will earn full interest from the beginning of the quarter.

• *How often is interest compounded?* The more frequently interest is compounded, the more you earn "interest on interest." The table below shows how a nominal annual rate of 5.25 percent would have a true annual rate of:

True Annual Rate (%)	If Compounded
5.3189	semiannually
5.3542	quarterly
5.3781	monthly
5.3874	weekly
5.3898	daily

Ideally, your savings should be in an *insured* savings institution that's *convenient* (near home or office), *offers all services you need*, pays interest from *day of deposit to day of withdrawal*, features *monthly grace days*, *compounds interest daily*, *pays quarterly*, and has the highest rate of interest.

You probably won't find everything in any one place. And also realize these important new regulations that went into effect July 1, 1979 that will affect your choice:

• *Higher interest rates.* Passbook rates on savings accounts have been raised to 5½% for savings banks and savings and loan associations and to 5¼% for commercial banks. Both types of institutions will also be allowed to issue new 30-month floating rate certificates paying a maximum rate of interest based on the rate of treasury securities of a similar maturity.

• *Early withdrawal penalties reduced.* On certificates of deposit issued or renewed after July 1, 1979, the penalty is limited to forfeiture of 3 months' interest if the CD matures in a year or less and 6 months' interest for longer maturities. This eliminates the reversion to passbook rates, which was the standard penalty for early withdrawal.

• *Minimum amounts.* These have been eliminated on the longer-term savings certificates, but the savings institutions can set their own limits. And banks and individuals may also *pool money* to buy $10,000 savings certificates tied to the current yield on 26-week Treasury bills.

The new regulations also allow savings institutions to issue *variable rate mortgages* with rates tied to an index.

Many savings and loan associations have special features that can give you more money on your savings. Among them are:

Where You Can Earn the Most Interest on Savings

• *Credit interest monthly*. Not only can you withdraw your interest monthly, you can place your funds in a 90-day notice account and—after the initial 90 days—withdraw funds and receive full interest. Among those that have offered this service:

- Majestic Savings & Loan, 1247 Pearl St., Boulder, CO 80302
- Home Federal Savings of the Rockies, 1531 North Lincoln, Loveland, CO 80537

• *Pay a bonus when funds aren't withdrawn*. Some savings and loans in southern California give you an extra ½% interest during any quarter in which funds are not withdrawn. Among those offering the plan:

- Mission Federal Savings, 936 State, Santa Barbara, CA 93102
- Santa Barbara Savings, 1035 State, Santa Barbara, CA 93102
- California Federal Savings, P.O. Box 54087, Terminal Annex, Los Angeles, CA 90054

You should also check mutual savings banks and thrift institutions (and some commercial banks) in New England and New York that offer NOW (Negotiable Orders of Withdrawal) accounts that pay interest like savings accounts but allow you to write checks against the account.

And remember that banks can now transfer funds automatically from your interest-bearing savings account to your checking account as needed. But to cover the added cost, most banks have raised their fees, so it's best to check what kind of savings-checking account is best for you.

In some cases you'd be better off in a nonprofit *credit union* that operates in conjunction with a corporation, church, club, college, labor union, etc. Rules have been liberalized so that *just about anyone* can be eligible to join a credit union. If you can't locate one near you, write *Credit Union National Association*, 1617 Sherman Ave., Madison, WI 53701. The credit unions usually pay highest rates on savings.

You could probably get about a 1% higher yield at *nonfederally insured* savings and loan associations. Most are state-controlled and

Higher Yield at "Offbeat" Savings Institutions

insured and offer protection similar to the Federal Savings & Loan Insurance Corporation—$40,000 maximum on accounts.

Here are some that accept deposits by mail; see what they have to offer:

- Surety Building & Loan, P.O. Box 819, DeLand, FL 32720
- Rio Grande Building & Loan, Box 2468, Harlingen, TX 78550
- Greater Baltimore S & L, 407 W. Saratoga St., Baltimore, MD 21201
- Friendship Savings & Loan, 5415 Friendship Blvd., Chevy Chase, MD 20015
- Security Savings & Loan, 102 St. Paul St., Baltimore, MD 21203
- Sharon Building & Loan, 232 N. Liberty St., Baltimore, MD 21201

You could also get almost 1% more interest at some *industrial banks* and *finance companies*. However, these accounts don't offer the insurance protection of other savings institutions, and the institutions may make "riskier" loans with your money.

You can find *industrial banks* by looking in the yellow pages of major metropolitan areas. And you can locate *finance companies* through the directory or by writing to the State Consumer Finance Association. You can obtain addresses by writing the National Consumer Finance Association, 1000 16th St., N.W., Washington, DC 20036.

Don't forget that the money-market funds discussed earlier offer a good alternative to savings accounts, and you can usually write checks against your account. The main point: whatever money you earmark for "savings" should be *safe* and *liquid* (you can get it easily). This is the money you need for *emergencies*—money you want immediately when you need it.

How To Make Money In Foreign Securities

Have a yen for yen? Want to make your mark with marks? You can exchange your dollars for any of several foreign currencies and/or foreign securities. But don't go rushing into overseas adventures until you understand the potential promise and pitfalls of such investments.

As some foreign securities—notably the Swiss franc, German mark, Japanese yen—are rising in value against the U.S. dollar, you could earn more money by investing in these currencies in the following ways:

• *Foreign currencies.* You can buy bank notes and travelers checks through the foreign currency departments of major banks or through major exchange brokers like Deak-Perera, 630 Fifth Ave., New York, NY (offices in many other major cities); Manfra, Tordella & Brookes, One World Trade Center, New York, NY 10048; Texas Foreign Exchange, P.O. Box 1400, Houston, TX 77081. Travelers checks usually are somewhat cheaper than banknotes, generally selling at about 1 to 1½% above the interbank middle rate (rate for large transactions). You can also buy these through American Express, Thomas Cook, or even by charging on a Diners Club card.

CURRENCY RATES

(In U.S. dollars)	
British pound	2.2010
Canadian dollar	0.8512
(In foreign units to U.S. dollar)	
French franc	4.0325
Japanese yen	239.65
Swiss franc	1.6020
West German mark	1.7295

Several foreign currencies (especially the Japanese yen, German mark, and Swiss franc) have risen in value against the sagging U.S. dollar, prompting many investors to exchange their dollars for the foreign monetary units. This chart reflects the relative value of the dollar vis-a-vis several currencies at the end of 1979.

• *Foreign bonds.* Foreign bonds yield between 3 and 6% (vs. 9% in the U.S.), but the real rate of return has been in capital gains against the U.S. dollar. In *total returns* (in dollars) here are some current foreign bond yields: Swiss (16½%), Germany (16%), Japan (14%), Netherlands (12%), United Kingdom (8%). Some bonds, such as the Swiss and Japanese, may be hard to buy, although a secondary market exists for them as well as for German and Dutch bonds. You may have to pay a tax on these bonds (although you can deduct them on your U.S. return), and you usually have to buy a minimum of $5,000 worth, although many corporate, World Bank, or European Investment bank bonds are available in smaller denominations. You can buy these bonds through the foreign bonds departments of large brokerage houses like Merrill Lynch. For bonds payable in Swiss francs issued by companies and governments from Austria to Denmark, France, Finland, Mexico, New Zealand, Norway, Sweden, and the U.S., write to Bankhaus Deak, Rathausstrasse 20, A-1010, Vienna, Austria.

• *Eurobonds.* These are medium and long-term bonds issued by corporations (U.S. and foreign), governments, and government agencies. Floated in third-country capital markets (outside of the issuers' national boundaries), they may or may not be denominated in the issuers' currency. Generally, Eurobonds are denominated in dollars (U.S. and Canadian), although they are also offered in other currencies, such as Swiss francs, German marks, Dutch guilders, etc. Some are traded on stock exchanges, such as those of Luxemburg, Frankfort, or London, but the most important trading facility for these issues are the secondary markets outside the United States. These bonds are usually in denominations of $1,000 (U.S.) and mature in 15 years or less. Any foreign withholding taxes depend upon the nationality of the issuer. You can find out about these and other Eurobonds by contacting major brokers such as Merrill Lynch. Here are current good buys, all rated *triple A* (highest) by Moody's and Standard & Poor, and all yielding around 10 percent or better:

- City of Stockholm 9¾, Mar. 15, 1994
- Kingdom of Norway 9¾, Jan. 15, 1984
- European Investment Bank 9⅞, Feb. 15, 1999
- Commonwealth of Australia 8⅞, Dec. 1, 1997
- Republic of Finland 9, Sept. 15, 1988
- European Investment Bank 9⅝, Feb. 15, 1986
- Lehman Bros. Multi-currency foreign bond fund

• *Foreign savings banks.* You can take advantage of the many services (and secrecy) offered foreign banks by opening accounts in Switzerland, Germany, Holland, Canada, and Mexico. While the interest rate may be low (as in Switzerland), you stand a chance of capital gains if the account is in the local currency. And any taxes paid abroad (up to 35% in some cases) can be taken as either a deduction from or credit again your federal return—if you itemize. Usually it's best to keep your foreign money outside the country that it's from (German marks in a Dutch bank; Swiss francs in a German bank, etc.) because some countries may try to limit foreign bank accounts, and you may have to pay quarterly charges. Here are some foreign banks to contact (some have branch offices in major U.S. cities):

Swiss
- Swiss Bank Corp., 4 World Trade Center, New York, NY 10048

- Swiss Credit Bank, 100 Wall St., New York, NY 10005
- Union Bank of Switzerland, 14 Wall St., New York, NY 10005

Dutch
- Algemene Bank Nederland, 84 Williams St., New York, NY 10038
- European-American Banking Corp., 10 Hanover Square, New York, NY 10005
- Slavenburg Corp., 1 Penn Plaza, New York, NY 10001
- Nederlandse Middenstands Bank, 450 Park Ave., New York, NY 10022

Canada
- Canadian Imperial Bank of Commerce, 22 William St., New York, NY 10005
- Canadian Bank of Commerce, 20 Exchange Place, New York, NY 10005
- Royal Bank of Canada, Royal Bank Plaza, Toronto, Ontario M5J 2J5

Mexico
- Banco Nacional de Mexico, S.A. 375 Park Ave., New York, NY 10022
- Banco Mexicano, S.A., 44 Wall St., New York, NY 10005
- Banamex, Isabel La Catolica 39, Mexico 1, D.F.
- Banca Metropolitana, Juarez 42B-3, Mexico 1, D.F.

- *International certificates of deposit.* For $5,000 or more you can buy international certificates of deposit yielding from 1 to 9%, depending upon the inverse strength of the currency (Swiss francs lowest; British pounds highest). To locate banks issuing ICS, contact local consulates to see which offers the best deal.
- *Foreign exchange futures.* Through the Chicago Mercantile Exchange (444 West Jackson Blvd., Chicago IL 60606) and the Commodity Exchange (4 World Trade Center, New York, NY 10048) you can buy international currency futures contracts—legal contracts for the purchase and receipt of a specified quantity of a specified currency at a definite future date at a specified price. See commodity brokers at leading brokerage houses for further information, or write the addresses above.
- *Foreign securities.* While the United States stock market compounded annual return (1959 to 1978) was a little over 6%, the total stock market annual rate of return (taking currency appreciation into account) was almost 18% in Japan, 13% in Switzerland, 12.7% in Ger-

many, 10% in Britain, 9% in both Canada and Australia, and over 8% in France. Through your broker you can buy shares of foreign companies (Swiss, German, Japanese) listed on the U.S. stock exchange as well as foreign stock exchanges. An alternative would be to invest in shares of *mutual funds* and *investment companies* that buy and sell a foreign company's shares on the company's national exchanges. Write for prospectuses from:

- The Canadian Fund, One Wall St., New York, NY 10005
- The Japan Fund, One Rockefeller Plaza, New York, NY 10020
- Scudder International Fund, 345 Park Ave., New York, NY 10022
- Templeton Growth Fund, 41 Beach Dr., St. Petersburg, FL 33701
- Templeton World Fund, 41 Beach Dr., St. Petersburg, FL 33701

Remember that exchange rates fluctuate daily, and there may be a time when the U.S. dollar will be stronger than Swiss francs, German marks, and the Japanese yen. So if you invest in any foreign-currency dominated securities, do so with *only* a small (less than 10 percent) part of your investment money, and then only as a hedge against further erosion of the U.S. dollar.

How Various Events Affect Investment Decisions

Interest rates, oil prices, presidential elections, labor strikes, upheavals overseas—the investment markets respond to all these important happenings. If you know how to anticipate the response, you can make money no matter whether the news is good or bad for the economy.

The investment markets not only reflect *what happens*. They often anticipate *what may happen*, and sometimes it takes them a while to respond to *what did happen*. For instance, during the last 6 recessions, interest rates peaked (on the average) *two months after the start* of the recession. The stock market hit bottom (on the average) *6 months after the start of the recession*. Yet, the stock market started rising (on the average) *5 months before* the recession ended.

Thus, markets both lagged behind events and anticipated events. Seldom did they reflect—absolutely—what was happening at the moment.

Keeping those caveats in mind, let's examine what *usually happens* to markets given the following events.

Rising interest rates *usually lower stock and bond prices*. The reason? The higher rates raise the yields on *new issues* of fixed income investments—U.S. Treasury bills, notes, and bonds; money-market funds; corporate and utility bonds; floating rate notes; municipal bonds, etc. Thus, these *new fixed-income issues* become more attractive investments. On the other hand, *lower* interest rates usually *raise* stock and bond prices because the stock market becomes a better place to invest, and older fixed-income issues also look more attractive. *The caveat:* in early to mid-1979, when the Federal Reserve raised the *discount rate* (the rate charged on loans from the central bank to commercial banks that are members of the Federal Reserve System) to 10½%, and the banks raised their prime rate to 12 percent, stock and bond prices actually rallied. The reason? More investors were afraid of inflation than they were afraid of higher interest rates, and they reasoned that the higher rates would *eventually* reduce inflation, lower interest rates, and cut borrowing costs. The better return on dollar investments attracted a lot of foreign money to both our stock and bond markets. Another factor: even late in 1979, when the prime rate was at 12% it was still *1% or more lower* than the inflation rate—and there was still strong demand to borrow money at what is essentially a "negative interest rate." However, *when and if interest rates top inflation rates*, then the reaction of the markets would be more predictable, with stock and bond prices *falling* with *higher rates; rising* with *lower rates.*

How Rising and Falling Interest Rates Affect Markets

As we discussed earlier, a 10% rise in oil prices adds about ½% to our inflation rate. Rising oil prices (paid in U.S. dollars) also weaken the dollar and strengthen gold prices, which mirror the strength of the dollar. Thus, it's more predictable to say that *rising oil prices will lower stock and bond prices, cause the dollar to drop in value,* and *raise gold prices*. Another danger with rising oil prices is that if the dollar sinks too low, the OPEC nations might demand payment in gold or some

How Hikes in Oil Prices Affect Investment Decisions

other "harder" currency (like the Swiss franc, German mark, or Japanese yen), and they could possibly *withdraw their dollars* from U.S. banks and other investments, thus causing near *economic collapse* of our system. This is a "worse case" scenario and is not likely to happen. But each rise in oil prices makes it *more likely to happen.*

How Presidential Elections Affect Investment Decisions

As was mentioned in Chapter 1, during a presidential election year, the Federal Reserve Board often "accommodates" an administration by *increasing the money supply,* thereby *lowering interest rates* and creating a general "favorable" economic climate with *rising stock and bond prices.* It happened when Arthur Burns (who supposedly was so independent) was Federal Reserve Board chairman, and it could happen again—especially if unemployment is high. About the only deterrent is if such a move would seriously damage the economy at a time when most everyone agreed that stimulus wasn't needed. However, if more money is made available and if interest rates are lowered, *the euphoria in the stock and bond prices would be short-lived.* The economy and administration would have to "sober up" after the election and take steps to control matters.

How Labor Strikes Affect Investment Decisions

Strikes usually *lower stock and bond prices.* Not only is the particular industry affected, but there's a "ripple effect" as other businesses that service the struck industry feel the pinch. Laid off workers and production cutbacks dry up consumer spending, and retail and other businesses and companies that depend upon discretionary spending also suffer. When the strike is settled, *the markets usually rise,* but this is often tempered by how inflationary is the settlement and what affect it will have on the economy in the long run. In summary: strikes are usually *bad news* for investment markets.

How Political-Economic Developments Oversees Affect Investment Decisions

The markets "hate uncertainty," and any political or economic upheaval usually causes *the markets to go down* unless some "obstacle" to peace and prosperity (such as an unpopular dictator) has been removed. Many American companies have overseas offices and branches, and those companies most exposed in the affected foreign country would see their stocks and bonds drop in price. Wars and economic upheavals usually *strengthen the price of gold and silver* and other "chaos hedges" but weaken the local currency, with possible ripple effects on other paper currencies. *After the upheaval is settled, stock and bond prices usually rise,* especially those companies who may get relief from the settlement or could prosper in any recovery programs.

The *housing* industry is usually hard-hit by an inflationary recession.

Building permits slow down, affecting the construction and such allied industries as cement, plywood, roofing and flooring materials, household equipment and appliances. *Mortgage money* dries up as high interest rates make mortgages more prohibitive. In many instances, *real estate prices drop* except in those areas where there's a shortage of housing or unusual demand. It's predicted that *housing in the Sunbelt* will *rise in price* as more people flee the cold winters and high heating bills of northern areas. Florida recently experienced a 22% rise in housing sales (while sales were dropping 20% nationwide) from northerners fleeing high housing and fuel costs. But, generally, housing is one of the first industries hurt by a recession and is often among the last to recover.

In strictly inflationary times, prices of collectibles *usually rise*, and people seek a refuge in more tangible assets. But in a *recession*, prices—except prices of those items that are truly rare and valuable— *usually drop* because people need money for necessities and can't "speculate" on collectibles. In an *inflationary-recession* prices on quality collectibles will *remain high*, while those of lesser quality will probably *drop*.

Gold and silver are not as good inflation hedges as they are "chaos hedges." There's an old saying about gold: "Buy when the cannons are booming; sell when the violins are playing." Gold is not an absolutely reliable inflation hedge because the retail price of gold tends to lag behind rises in the wholesale price level during inflationary periods. Gold historically has compensated for the lag and closed the gap with the price index during deflationary periods. The *net* result is that—*over the long term*—gold has been a good inflation hedge. However, in this inflationary-recession, the *industrial demand* for gold—and particularly for silver, which is primarily an industrial metal—will decline, causing a *slump in price*. This may be offset during the *Holiday season* (November through January) when the demand for *gold and silver jewelry* is at its peak. The best prognosis at this time: *lower short-term prices* but *rising long-term prices*.

If you have patience and are investing for the long-term, you can usually bet that the markets will *eventually respond to the realities of any situation. Stock and bond markets will drop when:*

- Interest rates rise
- Oil prices are hiked
- A major labor strike occurs
- A major political or economic upheaval takes place overseas.

How an Inflationary-Recession Will Affect Real Estate

How an Inflationary-Recession Will Affect Collectibles

How an Inflationary-Recession Affects Gold-Silver Prices

How to Make Money When These Events Occur

110

And, of course, they will *rise* when the reverse takes place.
Gold and silver prices and those of *quality collectibles* will rise:

- When the dollar declines
- When a major political or economic upheaval threatens almost anywhere
- If oil-producing nations want payment in gold or other tangible assets
- When the stock and bond markets are low
- When real estate investments dry up.

Six Model Portfolios In An Inflationary Recession

Here are six model portfolios of $10,000, one each for young singles, young heads of households, developing families, maturing families, retired couples, and widows or widowers. All include something for savings, something for guaranteed income, and something to keep ahead of inflation.

Earlier in this book, we offered the following advice about determining the amount of risk you can take. Generally, the younger you are and/or the more money you have, the more risks you can take and the easier you can replace lost money. The older you are and/or the less money you have, the more you should stress *safety* and *income* to meet current needs. As we also mentioned, all of us have these three basic categories of need: *savings* for emergencies, *guaranteed income* to meet expenses, and *investment income* to keep ahead of inflation.

We compared various investments in each of these categories and gave you a *Profile Analysis* that would help you pinpoint the types of investments you should be mainly concerned with. However, we tempered this with the suggestion that you should *keep financial plans flexible* in the face of *changing economic conditions*. As you probably noted in the table "Various Investment Climates" we are in *climate #5: Stormy and windy with little letup in sight*. Inflation and interest rates recently have been at new highs with no real relief in sight. We suggest that for a *growth* strategy we would retain stress on liquidity; buy options in 8 to 12-month range; maintain a gold hedge. For an *income* strategy we would move to longer-term maturities at high interest rates and buy call options.

Keeping these strategies in mind, let's develop *six model portfolios* of $10,000 each for these groups: (1) young singles; (2) young heads of households; (3) developing families; (4) maturing families; (5) retired couples; (6) widows (or widowers).

At this age and stage of living, you're most interested in "instant gratification": dreams of adventurous vacations and travel, entertaining sports and games, sexual freedom—with perhaps vague "responsible" thoughts of getting married—and starting a career.

A Portfolio for Young Singles

Here's where the single might put his or her money:

Investment Goal	Amount	Best Possible Places to Meet Goal
Savings	$1,000	*Money-market funds* like Reserve Fund, Scudder Managed Reserves, Fidelity Cash Reserves, Federated Money Market
Guaranteed	$1,000	*Deep-discount, high-yielding bond funds* like Oppenheimer High Yield, Fidelity Aggressive Income, Keystone B-4, Putnam High Yield.
Inflation	$8,000	*Aggressive* growth stocks like Baker International, Data General, Digital Equipment, General Instruments, Mesa Petroleum, Tektronix, Tiger International, Waste Management; or *aggressive stock funds* like AMCAP, Charter Fund, Fidelity Destiny, 44 Wall, Nicholas Fund, the Japan Fund, Templeton Growth; *high-yielding gold-mining stocks* like President Brand, President Steyn, Western Deep Levels, Western Holding, Vaal Reefs. Also consider gold and silver bullion, rare coins, options, futures; *collectibles* in some field you're knowledgeable in.

A Portfolio for Young Heads of Households

This is the "striving and arriving" decade when you want to increase both the savings and earnings on your investments. However, your major emphasis still is on inflation protection not only for current needs but to meet large bills for education, etc., in the future.

Here's what your portfolio might look like, assuming there is only one breadwinner in a family with one or two pre-school children.

Investment Goal	Amount	Best Possible Places to Meet Goal
Savings	$1,500	Capital-preservation funds like Capital Preservation, American Fund of Government Securities, Fund of U.S. Government Securities.
Guaranteed	$1,500	Intermediate & longer bond funds like Northeast Investors Trust, Rowe Price, New Income, or closed-end bond funds like John Hancock Income, InterCapital Income, Montgomery St. Income. Good discount bonds like those of Bell System
Inflation	$7,000	Above-average appreciation stocks like AMAX, Burlington Northern, Diamond Shamrock, RCA, Southern Natural Resources, Wheelbrator Frey. No-load mutual stock funds like ContraFund, Financial Industrial Income, Guardian Mutual, Twentieth Century Growth, Windsor Fund. Real estate (family home). Gold bullion coins like Kruger-rands, Mexican 50 Peso, Austrian 100 Corona. Collectibles like prints, stamps, rare coins.

This is the decade of midlife crisis, shifting gears, physical and psychological "menopause." At this point you need more *safety* and *emergency* investments to cover crisis. Yet your emphasis is still on inflation protection, although you need to *increase income* to meet rising current expenses.

Investment Goal	*Amount*	*Best Possible Places to Meet Goal*
Emergency	$2,000	*Highest insured* credit unions, savings banks and savings and loans, perhaps split with *capital preservation funds* like Capital Preservation or Mutual of Omaha America.
Guaranteed	$1,000	*Mortgage unit trusts* or *mutual funds* like Holdings of U.S. Government Securities. *Convertible bond funds* like American General Convertibles, Bancroft Convertible, Chase Convertible. Floating rate notes.
Inflation	$7,000	*Established growth stocks* like American Electric Power, Abbott Laboratories, Bristol-Myers, Exxon, Household Finance, Southern Pacific, Tampa Electric, United Telecomm. *Quality growth mutual funds* like David L. Babson Investment, Johnston Mutual, T. Rowe Price Growth, Putnam Investors. *Gold-mining securities* like Rosario Resources, ASA Ltd., Anglo-American or *gold and silver mining mutual funds* like International Investors and United Services. *Income-producing real estate.* *Collectibles* like art and antiques.

Portfolio for Maturing Families

This is the "nailing down" decade when you are winding up past goals and are settling down for the future. Your earnings may be at a peak, but so are expenses for college educations, marriages, etc. This should also be the nest egg–building stage for retirement.

Investment Goal	Amount	Best Possible Places to Meet Goal
Emergency	$2,500	*Insured* savings accounts in leading commercial or savings banks. Only federally-chartered credit unions.
Guaranteed	$2,500	*High-quality corporate and utility bonds* like those of the Bell systems and leading oil companies. Some *state and local municipal bonds* rated A or better. Perhaps *bonds hinged to oil, gold, foreign currencies.*
Inflation	$5,000	*High-quality stocks* with *above-average yields*: American Brands, American Can, Carolina Power & Light, Chemical New York, Commonwealth Edison, Mountain States Telephone, Northern States Power, Standard Oil of California, Texaco, Tenneco, Union Carbide. *High-quality closed-end stock funds* like Asset Investors, General American, the Lehman Corporation, Niagara Corporation. *Balanced funds* like Kemper Total Return, Vance Sanders, Loomis-Sayles, Stein Roe & Farnham. *Real estate* (second or vacation home rented when not in use). *Collectibles* like rare books, manuscripts, autographs.

This is the true "settling in" decade when people make final plans for the rest of their lives. Hopefully, family responsibilities and expenses are behind, and a lifetime of leisure is ahead. Income may be less but so are expenses. However, the emphasis is now on *income* and *safety* and less on growth and inflation protection. Here are some investment suggestions for people in their sixties:

Portfolio for Retirement Couple

Investment Goal	Amount	Best Possible Places to Meet Goal
Emergency	$3,000	*Insured* commercial banks of highest-quality. *Time deposits* if withdrawal penalty is not too severe. *U.S. Treasury bills* if kept to 3-month minimum (available through Capital Preservation fund for $1,000 minimum investment).
Guaranteed	5,000	*U.S. Treasury notes* with 2 to 4 year maturity. *High-quality corporate bonds* from AT&T, Ford Motor Credit, General Motors Acceptance, United Technologies. *Annuity income* from investment annuities and other annuities. *Municipal bond unit trusts* of AA-rated bonds of states and localities.
Inflation	2,000	*Highest quality common stocks* like AT&T, Central & So. West, Charter new York, New England Electric, Household Finance, Mobil Oil, Tampa Electric, F. W. Woolworth. *High-quality utility stocks* (besides those already mentioned): Citizens Utilities, Consolidated Edison, Florida Power & Light, Public Service Indiana, S. California Edison, Texas Utilities, Tucson Electric Power. *Balanced funds* like Kemper Total Return, Vance Sanders.

Portfolio for Widows or Widowers

Most women will end up single; at age 65 there are 143 women over age 65 for every 100 men. And because women outlive men by about 8 years and because men often marry younger women, it's not unusual for a woman to outlive her husband by some 20 years. At this stage and age of living *one can't take chances*. All investments should be there to *generate income* with *maximum safety*. Here's how such a portfolio might look:

Investment Goal	*Amount*	*Best Possible Places to Meet Goal*
Emergency	$4,000	Only *insured savings accounts* of highest quality. Passbook accounts or 1-year maximum time deposits.
Guaranteed	$5,000	*Straight life or charitable annuities; U.S. Treasury notes or bonds;* withdrawal plan of U.S. Fund for Government Securities or American Fund of Government securities. Perhaps *federal agency issues* that are implied or direct obligations of the U.S. government like Federal National Mortgage Association, Government National Mortgage Association, Federal Land Bank, TWA. Perhaps *highest* grade municipal bonds of state.
Inflation	$1,000	*Highest rated* common stocks like AT&T, Mobil Corp., Royal Dutch Petroleum, Central & South West, Tampa Electric. Perhaps *balanced funds* like Kemper Total Return or Union Income.

Beyond The Recession: How Continuing Inflation Will Affect Your Future

The next few years look grim indeed as far as the economy is concerned. But if you follow the suggestions in this book, you should have enough money to pay your bills *and* stay ahead of inflation.

The outlook isn't good—neither short nor long term. Taking the longer view first, here is how inflation will affect your money needs, assuming a *modest continuing inflation* of only 6% annually:

Today	5 Years	10 Years	15 Years	30 Years
$1,000	$1,338	$1,791	$3,207	$5,745

Assuming that same rate of inflation, here are how your money needs might look in the year 2001 assuming you need $10,000 a year now to meet basic living costs:

Item	Percent / Cost	Need in 2001
Rent	20 / $2,000	$8,600
Food	20 / 2,000	8,600
Clothing	15 / 1,500	6,450
Utilities	3 / 300	1,290
Health care	7 / 700	3,010
Savings	5 / 500	2,150
Auto	10 / 1,000	4,300
Household upkeep	10 / 1,000	4,300
Entertainment	10 / 1,000	4,300

You'll have a tough job just staying even—a harder one keeping ahead. Now, focusing on the shorter view: *Over the next year* we predict *continuing high interest rates* and *prices, deepening unemployment,* and *slowing economic growth.* We expect the *stock and bond markets to hit a low* some time during the winter. However, *the markets should rise during the spring* due to the Federal Reserve loosening money and *lowering the interest rates* to create a more favorable "pre-election climate."

When this happens, you can *sell* some of your money-market investments and other short-term fixed income investments and *start buying* stocks and bonds.

No matter who wins the 1980 presidential election, there will be a "sobering up" around January 1981 when the market responds to the realities—which will probably mean *continuing high inflation.* Whether or not the Federal Reserve Board will have the courage to hike interest rates back up remains to be seen; with the election out of the way, chances would be improved. If that happens, *sell your stocks and bonds* on a rising market, and start putting your money back into *U.S. Treasury bills, money-market funds,* and other short-term (under 1-year) *fixed income investments* or, perhaps, *floating rate notes.*

Throughout these times, maintain a *hedge* (10 to 25% of investments) in *gold, silver, real estate, quality collectibles. Inflation is a way of life* in America, and there's nothing on the horizon that suggests otherwise.

But if you follow the suggestions in this book, you should not only have enough money to *pay your bills today,* but enough money to *stay ahead of inflation tomorrow.*

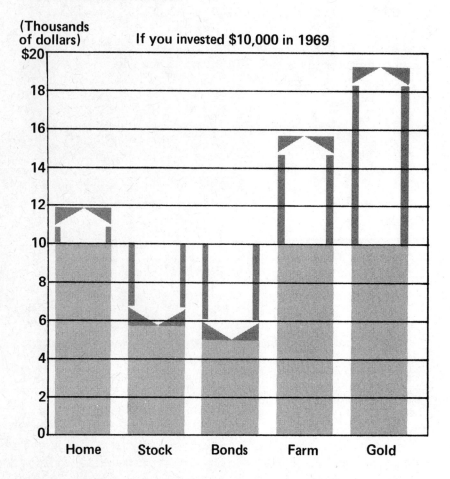

(Thousands of dollars)

If you invested $10,000 in 1969

An investor who ten years ago put his money in farmland and gold would be far ahead of a colleague who relied on the stock and bond markets to stay ahead of inflation. The homeowner also scored a victory, though a relatively modest one, over inflation.

Source Directory

Algemene Bank Nederland, 105
84 Williams Street
New York, NY 10038
Contact regarding foreign securities

American Art & Antiques, 86
1515 Broadway
New York, NY 10036
Contact regarding information on antiques

American Board of Trade, 26
286 Fifth Avenue
New York, NY 10001
Contact regarding investing in silver bullion

The American Collector's Journal, 86, 94
P.O. Box 1431
Porterville, CA 93258
Contact regarding selling antiques

The American Crafts Council, 95
44 West 53rd Street
New York, NY
Contact regarding information on selling crafts

American Fund of Government Securities, 41, 53
P.O. Box 9650
San Francisco, CA 94120
Contact regarding investing in U.S. government securities

American General Convertible Securities, 41, 63
c/o SISCOR
P.O. Box 24226
Los Angeles, CA 90024
Contact regarding convertible funds

American Insurance & Industrial, 42
4333 Edgewood Road, NE
Cedar Rapids, IA 52406
Contact regarding insurance funds

American Investors and Income Funds, 39, 59
88 Field Point Road
Greenwich, CT 06830
Contact regarding mutual funds and bond funds

American Numismatic Association, 88

P.O. Box 2366
Colorado Springs, CO 80901
Contact regarding information on collecting coins

American Numismatic Society, 88
617 West 155th Street
New York, NY 10032
Contact regarding information on collecting coins

American Philatelic Society, 92
P.O. Box 800
State College, PA 16801
Contact regarding stamp authentication

American Society of Appraisers, 83, 94
60 East 42nd Street
New York, NY 10017
Contact regarding information on appraisals

The American Stamp Dealers Association, 92
595 Madison Avenue
New York, NY 10022

The page number(s) following the name of the source refers to where it appears in the text.

Contact regarding information on stamp collecting

Anchor National Life Insurance, 79
Anchor National Life Plaza
Camelback at 22nd Street
Phoenix, AZ 85016
Contact regarding annuities

Antiquarian Booksellers Center, 90
50 Rockefeller Plaza
New York, NY 10020
Contact regarding antique book dealers

Antique Monthly, 86
Boone, Inc.
Drawer 2
Tuscaloosa, AL 35401
Contact regarding information on antiques

Antiques, 86
551 Fifth Avenue
New York, NY 10017
Contact regarding information on antiques

The Appraisers Association of America, 83, 94
541 Lexington Avenue
New York, NY 10022
Contact regarding information on appraisals

The Art Dealers Association of America, 86, 95
575 Madison Avenue
New York, NY 10022
Contact regarding information on art dealers

ASA Ltd., 41
P.O. Box 1724
FDR Station
New York, NY 10022
Contact regarding information on gold funds

Baker & Co., Inc, 44
1801 E. Ninth Street
Cleveland, OH 44114
Contact regarding discount brokers

Baker, Fentress & Co., 42
208 LaSalle Street
Chicago, IL 60604
Contact regarding specialty funds

B. D. Harmer, 92
6 West 48th Street

New York, NY 10036
Contact regarding auctions

Banamex, 105
Isabel La Catolica 39
Mexico 1, D.F.
Contact regarding foreign securities

Banca Metropolitana, 105
Juraez 42B-3
Mexico 1, D.F.
Contact regarding foreign securities

Banco Mexicano, S.A., 105
44 Wall Street
New York, NY 10005
Contact regarding foreign securities

Banco Nacional de Mexico, S.A, 105
375 Park Avenue
New York, NY 10022
Contact regarding foreign securities

Bancroft Convertible Fund, 41, 63
660 Madison Avenue
New York, NY 10021
Contact regarding convertible funds

Bankhaus Deak, 104
Pathausstrasse 20,
A-1010
Vienna, Austria
Contact regarding foreign securities

Bayrock Advisors, Inc., 43
100 Gold Street
New York, NY 10038
Contact regarding investment information

Bramble Coins, 22
1604 Michigan National Tower
Lansing, MI 48933
(800) 248-5952 (or in Michigan) (517) 484-3198
Contact regarding gold coin dealers

Bureau of the Public Debt, 52
Securities Transactions Branch
RM. 2134—U.S. Treasury Building
Washington, DC 20226
Contact regarding information on U.S. government securities

California Federal Savings,, 100
P.O. Box 54087
Terminal Annex
Los Angeles, CA 90054
Contact regarding bonus payments on savings accounts

Canadian Bank of Commerce, 105

20 Exchange Place
New York, NY 10005
Contact regarding foreign securities

The Canadian Fund, 42, 106
One Wall Street
New York, NY 10005
Contact regarding foreign company investments and foreign fund investments

Canadian Imperial Bank of Commerce, 105
22 Williams Street
New York, NY 10005
Contact regarding foreign securities

Capital Life, 80
1600 Sherman Street
Denver, CO 80201
Contact regarding annuities

Capital Preservation Fund, 47, 53
459 Hamilton Avenue
Palo Alto, CA 94301
Contact regarding money-market funds

Century Shares, 42
111 Devonshire Street
Boston, MA 02109
Contact regarding insurance funds

Charles Schwab & Co., 44
120 Montgomery Street
San Francisco, CA 94104
Contact regarding discount brokers

Chase Convertible Fund of Boston, 41
535 Boylston St.
Boston, MA 02116
Contact regarding convertible funds

Chicago Board of Trade, 27
141 W. Jackson Blvd.
Chicago, IL 60604
Contact regarding silver futures

Chicago Board Options Exchange, 41
141 W. Jackson Blvd.
Chicago, IL 60604
Contact regarding options

Chicago Mercantile Exchange, 23, 105
444 West Jackson Blvd.
Chicago, IL 60606
Contact regarding foreign exchange futures and gold futures contracts

First Investment Annuity of America, 79
Valley Forge Executive Mall
P.O. Box 831
Valley Forge, PA 19482
Contact regarding annuities

The Franklin Mint, 27
Franklin Center, PA 19063
Contact regarding silver art

Friendship Savings and Loan, 101
5415 Friendship Blvd.
Chevy Chase, MD 20015
Contact regarding information on non-federally insured institutions

Fund for U.S. Government Securities, 41, 53
421 Seventh Avenue
Pittsburgh, PA 15219
Contact regarding investing in U.S. government securities

Gem Hedge International, 77
440 Park Avenue S.
New York, NY 10016
Contact regarding information on specialty IRA accounts

The Gemological Institute, 89
580 Fifth Avenue
New York, NY 10036
Contact regarding diamond certification

The Gemological Institute, 89
1660 Stewart Street
Santa Monica, CA 90404
Contact regarding diamond certification

Golconda Investors, 41
111 Broadway
New York, NY 10006
Contact regarding investing in gold funds

Greater Baltimore Savings and Loan, 101
407 Saratoga Street
Baltimore, MD 21201
Contact regarding information on non-federally insured institutions

Growth Industry Shares, 39
135 LaSalle Street
Chicago, IL 60603
Contact regarding mutual funds

Guardian Mutual Fund, 39

522 Fifth Avenue
New York, NY 10036
Contact regarding mutual funds

Harbor Fund, 42, 63
c/o SISCOR
P.O. Box 24226
Los Angeles, CA 90024
Contact regarding convertible funds

High Yield Securities, 60
1080 Dresser Tower
Houston, TX 77002
Contact regarding discount bond funds

Holdings of U.S. Government Securities (HUSGSI), 74
3200 Ponce de Leon Blvd.
Coral Gables, FL 33134
Contact regarding mortgage investments

Home Federal Savings of the Rockies, 100
1531 North Lincoln
Loveland, CO 80537
Contact regarding monthly credit interest

Hornblower Asset Management Corp., 43
14 Wall Street
New York, NY 10005
Contact regarding investment information

Intercapital Liquid Assets, 48
One Battery Park
New York, NY 10004
Contact regarding money market funds

International Investors, 25
122 E. 42nd Street
New York, NY 10017
Contact regarding investing in gold mining stocks

Investment Company Institute, 39
1775 K Street, NW
Washington, DC 20006
Contact regarding mutual fund member firms

Investor Service Bureau, 43
New York Stock Exchange
P.O. Box 252
New York, NY 10005
Contact regarding investment information

Ivy Fund, 39
28 State Street
Boston, MA 02109
Contact regarding mutual funds

The Japan Fund, 42, 106
One Rockefeller Plaza
New York, NY 10020
Contact regarding foreign securities and foreign funds

Johnston Mutual Fund, 39
245 Park Avenue
New York, NY 10017
Contact regarding mutual funds

Kemper High Yield and Money Market Fund, 48, 60, 62
120 S. LaSalle Street
Chicago, IL 60603
Contact regarding discount bond funds, money market funds, and municipal bond funds

Keystone B-4, 60
99 High Street
Boston, MA 02110
Contact regarding discount bond funds

The Lapidary Journal, 90
3564 Kettner Blvd.
San Diego, CA 92138
Contact regarding information on diamonds

Lehman Management Co., 63
55 Water Street
New York, NY 10041
Contact regarding foreign bond funds

Letterman Transaction Services, 44
19742 MacArthur Blvd.
Irvine, CA 92715
Contact regarding discount brokers

Life Insurance Investors, 42
170 Fourth Avenue, N
Nashville, TN 27319
Contact regarding insurance funds

Life Insurance of Georgia, 80
600 W. Peachtree Street, NW
Atlanta, GA 30308
Contact regarding annuities

Linn's Weekly Stamp News, 92
911 Vandemark Road
P.O. Box 150
Sidney, OH 45365

120 Wall Street
New York, NY 10005
Contact regarding discount brokers

Research Equity Fund, 41
155 Bovet Road
San Mateo, CA 94402
Contact regarding gold funds

RET Income Fund, 41
One Winthrop Square
Boston, MA 02210
Contact regarding real estate funds

Rio Grande Building and Loan, 101
Box 2468
Houston, TX 78550
*Contact regarding non-federally
insured institutions*

Rose & Co., 44
Board of Trade Building
Chicago, IL 60604
Contact regarding discount brokers

Rowe Price, 39, 48, 59, 62
100 E. Pratt Street
Baltimore, MD 21202
*Contact regarding bond funds,
money market finds, municipal bond
funds, and mutual funds*

Royal Bank of Canada, 105
Royal Bank Plaza
Toronto, Ontario M5J 2J5
Contact regarding foreign securities

S.-G. Securities, 41
One Boston Place
Boston, MA 02108
Contact regarding real estate funds

Santa Barbara Savings, 100
1035 State
Santa Barbara, CA 93102
*Contact regarding bonus payments
on savings accounts*

Scott Publishing Co., 77, 92
3 East 57th Street
New York, NY 10022
*Contact regarding specialty IRA
accounts*

Scudder Funds, 39, 48, 62
175 Federal Street
Boston, MA 02110
*Contact regarding money market
funds, municipal bond funds, and
mutual funds*

**Scudder International and
Development Funds,** 42, 106
345 Park Avenue
New York, NY 10022
*Contact regarding foreign funds,
foreign securities, and specialty
funds*

Security Savings and Loan, 101
102 St. Paul Street
Baltimore, MD
*Contact regarding non-federally
insured institutions*

Sharon Building & Loan, 101
232 N. Liberty Street
Baltimore, MD 21201
*Contact regarding non-federally
insured institutions*

Silver Institute, 27
1001 Connecticut Avenue, NW
Washington, DC 20036
*Contact regarding investing in silver
coins*

Slavenburg Corp., 105
1 Penn Plaza
New York, NY 10001
Contact regarding foreign securities

Sotheby Parke Bernet, 86, 92, 94
980 Madison Avenue
New York, NY 10021
*Contact regarding information on art
dealers and auctions*

Source Securities Corp., 44
70 Pine Street
New York, NY 10005
Contact regarding discount brokers

Spear and Staff, 43
Babson Park, MA 02157
*Contact regarding investment
assistance*

**Springer Investment & Securities
Co.,** 44
6060 North College
Indianapolis, IN 46220
Contact regarding discount brokers

The Stamp Market Report, 92
P.O. Box 1328
Jackson, NY 08527
*Contact regarding information on
stamp collecting*

Swiss Bank Corp., 104

4 World Trade Center
New York, NY 10048
Contact regarding foreign securities

Swiss Credit Bank, 105
100 Wall Street
New York, NY 10005
Contact regarding foreign securities

**Templeton Growth and World
Fund,** 42, 106
41 Beach Drive
St. Petersburg, FL 33701
*Contact regarding foreign securities
and foreign funds*

Texas Foreign Exchange, 103
P.O. Box 1400
Houston, TX 77081
*Contact regarding foreign
currencies*

Thrift Trading, Inc, 44
223 Northstar Center
Minneapolis, MN 55402
Contact regarding discount brokers

Union Bank of Switzerland, 105
14 Wall Street
New York, NY 10005
Contact regarding foreign securities

United Services Fund, 25, 41
110 E. Bryd
Universal City, TX
*Contact regarding gold funds and
gold mining stocks*

U.S. Savings Bond Division, 54
Treasury Department
Washington, DC 20206
*Contact regarding information on
U.S. savings bonds*

**Value Line Development Capital
Corp.,** 42
Five E. 44th Street
New york, NY 10017
Contact regarding specialty funds

W. T. Cabe & Co., 44
1270 Avenue of the Americas
New York, NY 10020
Contact regarding discount brokers

Windsor Fund, 39
P.O. Box 1100
Valley Forge, PA 19482
Contact regarding mutual funds